The History of the Fellowship of Christian Assemblies

Dr. Warren Heckman

Published in Beaverton, Oregon, by Good Book Publishing.
www.goodbookpublishing.com
V1.1

Printed in the United States of America

Table of Contents

Prologue
By Dr. Warren Heckman

While attending a denominational Bible college in the late 1950s, I met one of my favorite teachers, who taught church history. He would wax eloquent in his admiration for that particular Pentecostal denomination and would denigrate those of lesser size and prominence, usually concluding by saying most of them were cultish, with unsound doctrine and practices. The funny thing was, as his student, I could tell I was almost his "teacher's pet," because he knew I was working full time at night loading freight trucks and taking a full college load and getting all A's. It was a very difficult schedule.

Finally, after hearing yet another nasty criticism about these little questionable groups that should be done away with, I approached him at the end of class, and in fear and trembling said, "Dr., I don't belong to your Pentecostal denomination. I belong to the Fellowship of Christian Assemblies (then known as Independent Assemblies of God), and we are not a cult, and our doctrine is the same as yours, except for our lack of denominational organization." At that time his denomination was struggling with the problem of organizational politics and control. Power struggles and personalities were in conflict with each other. Perhaps our lack of organization as a group was appealing.

The History of the FCA

He was shocked. It was as if I had hit him square on the jaw. He got red-faced and apologized profusely and asked me to forgive him.

I said, "It's okay."

Weeks later in class, he was speaking faster than his brain was registering, and he again blasted those little upstart groups with their questionable... Suddenly, he stopped, looked at me, smiled and said, "Of course there are exceptions, and some are very good." He was a good man and a great teacher.

It seemed to me that his denomination was struggling with the challenge of organizational politics; in other words, control from the top down, powerful personalities taking over and forcing their will on others. Perhaps our lack of organization was appealing. Also, as a small denomination, the FCA and others often operate under the radar. If known, they are often looked at suspiciously as being unorthodox and cultish.

When I clarified our doctrinal position and historical background, he understood us better and defended us, like in class that day.

Purpose
By Dr. Warren Heckman

Solomon's words echo in my mind: "To everything there is a season, and a time to every purpose under heaven" (Ecclesiastes 3:1 KJV). Season, time and purpose converge in a united motivation, prompting me to attempt this project.

I am in the latter season of my life and ministry. The Fellowship of Christian Assemblies (FCA) is now being led by the Baby Buster-Gen X generation. Many have asked about our (the FCA's) past, our history, what has shaped our thinking, our strong convictions regarding Ecclesiology (local church sovereignty) and why we do things the way we do. So, I felt it was time to research our past and try to understand our roots. I wrote the original manuscript to fulfill certain requirements for a master's degree in church management from Olivet Nazarene University. But it has been fueled by a personal desire to study our FCA history, and now we publish it in book form for you to glean from our rich heritage.

As I write this from my heart, it has stirred deep emotions within me. Our forefathers paid a huge price in pioneering the Pentecostal movement at the turn of the century. Their rigid stand for local church autonomy was forged out of the fire of persecution. They experienced rejection and loss of family, friends and denominational acceptance when they embraced this new Pentecostal teaching. In studying scripture, they saw New Testament churches functioning without external denominational organizational control. They strongly embraced such doctrinal teaching. This has impacted the FCA to this day.

My attempts at objectivity are clouded by my strong personal feelings of love and appreciation for all those presently in the FCA and for those who have carried this torch before me. Yet, at the same time, my strong personal desire to see us look forward, move forward and cooperatively accomplish more stir me to write critically of our foibles, egocentricities and weaknesses. While this is an attempt to trace the history of the FCA, I have attempted to keep this information to a minimum.

The Short Version

The Fellowship of Christian Assemblies is a family of autonomous evangelical churches with Pentecostal convictions.

This movement was born out of a special outpouring of the Holy Spirit in the United States and other countries at the turn of the previous century. Its participants welcomed the infilling and gifts of the Holy Spirit, as seen in the life of the early Church. Numerous local churches formed for the purpose of worship and mission with an openness to the ministry of the Spirit.

Roots of the movement can be traced at least in part to the Wesleyan-holiness renewal and the "Deeper Life" emphases of the late 1800s. Wesleyans emphasized a definite sanctification experience, and Deeper Life advocates stressed an empowerment of the Spirit for witness and service.

In addition, the Fellowship of Christian Assemblies points to other sources which are strongly Baptist, particularly in the area of local church structure.

In 1906, an outbreak of the Holy Spirit occurred among Scandinavian Baptists in Chicago, Illinois. About that time, William F. Durham, also of Baptist heritage, saw gifts of the Spirit in his North Avenue Mission. Durham soon became the leading non-Wesleyan voice in the early movement.

His "finished work of Christ" theme claimed that the

door to God's gifts was open to all believers immediately upon professing their faith in Christ. Durham affected future Pentecostal leaders in the United States and Canada, including a group of ministers who would eventually form what they called the Scandinavian Independent Assemblies of God.

Among them were Bengt Magnus Johnson, who brought from his Baptist background a vigorous stand on local-church autonomy; A.A. Holmgren, of the same heritage; and Gunnar Wingren, who pioneered the great work in Brazil. Also included was Arthur F. Johnson, whose service would continue into the future Fellowship of Christian Assemblies.

Meanwhile in Canada, Scandinavians were influenced as early as 1908 by Christina Larson, who brought the Pentecostal message from her native Norway to the small town of Weldon, Saskatchewan. In these pioneer days, meetings were held in homes, schools and even barns. Contact with other groups was encouraged, however, through the efforts of Carl O. Nordin of Amisk, Alberta, among others. He even made contact with like-minded leaders across the border in the United States.

Arthur F. Johnson became mentor to Elmer C. Erickson, whose ministry at the Duluth Gospel Tabernacle in northern Minnesota over four decades was a primary course-setting influence in the fellowship. Johnson and Erickson concentrated on English-speaking ministries, while maintaining contact with two ethnic groups, the Scandinavian Independent Assemblies of God and the

The Short Version

Scandinavian Assemblies of God. In 1922 in St. Paul, Minnesota, about 25 ministers from these three groups decided to come under a common, informal banner — the Independent Assemblies of God, an unincorporated fellowship.

A major concern of this new fellowship was local-church autonomy. A strong emphasis upon self-governing local churches had marked the early stages of the Pentecostal renewal. The nascent Independent Assemblies of God were determined to retain that stance.

By 1935, the fellowship listed 54 pastors and evangelists and 21 foreign missionaries. Five years later, their ranks had grown to 160.

Lewi Pethrus, pastor of the noted Filadelfia Church in Stockholm, Sweden, influenced the fellowship through his visits and writings on "assembly life." E.C. Erickson launched *Herald of Faith* magazine in 1936. The group's first national convention was held that year in Brooklyn, New York. For several years, annual national conferences alternated between Duluth and Chicago. Regional and area conferences proliferated, providing a glue for the fellowship.

On the Canadian side, Ole Forseth was instrumental in bringing A.W. Rasmussen to conduct meetings at Bethel Pentecostal Church in the Peace River area of Alberta in the early 1940s. Pastor Rasmussen saw the need for a central gathering point to rally the many small groups, and so he moved his family to Edmonton in 1945. Edmonton Gospel Temple was established the next year.

The History of the FCA

He was soon joined by T.E. Crane, and together they founded Temple Bible College. The Edmonton church hosted conventions twice a year, in the spring and the fall. Eventually, as other churches were planted, the conventions moved around the country and settled on a once-a-year schedule.

During the period up to 1950, the fellowship was fairly informal in its pursuit of Pentecostal experience combined with local-church autonomy and evangelism. Turmoil during the so-called "Latter Rain" movement of the late 1940s stimulated a quest for clearer identity and more cohesive practical cooperation. The ministerial listing process was strengthened. A new magazine, *Conviction* (later renamed *Fellowship Today*), was launched in 1963. The working process of the fellowship was defined in a brochure in 1959, and a new name, Fellowship of Christian Assemblies, was adopted in 1973.

Ministerial development was enhanced by Bible colleges in or alongside local churches, not only in Edmonton but also Seattle Bible College, founded by Philadelphia Church, Seattle (led by Roy Johnson) and Chicago Bible College (later Christian Life College), launched by Philadelphia Church, Chicago. Leadership in home and foreign missions continued strong across the fellowship.

With the eventual passing of its father figures, the fellowship turned increasingly toward task forces and other collegial means for leadership in projects. National convention planning committees prepared for events at conference centers or local churches. In addition to the general convention, a smaller mid-year Fellowship Concerns Conference, open to all, was conceived, to probe matters of theological and practical concern and to enable discussions at the grass-roots level. To this day, the fellowship affirms the two strands of local-church autonomy and inter-church responsibility.

Statements of Nature and Mission and Common Beliefs were adopted in a joint U.S.-Canadian conference at Banff, Alberta, in 1986. The mission statement affirms our Pentecostal heritage and views the Great Commission as the overarching purpose for our existence as a group of churches.

In 2000, the U.S. group voted to incorporate itself as "an association of autonomous local churches," setting up bylaws, empowering an official board and appointing a national coordinator.

Definitions of membership requirements, expectations, relationships and accountability were spelled out. Each member church was asked to support the fellowship with 0.25 percent of its general-fund income.

In 2007, the Canadian group made structural adjustments of its own, establishing five Fellowship Elders to give guidance and counsel to the churches and ministers. A National Committee of Pastors was organized along geographical lines to maintain ties in the various regions.

The American and Canadian groups now list nearly the same number of churches — about 100 each. Though

The History of the FCA

the Scandinavian flavor has faded with the passing years, the passion for Spirit-led worship and effective evangelism remains at the core of the FCA.

Perspectives from Current Board Members

In 1982, I was sent out to plant a church where I grew up in Brentwood, New York (on Long Island). My pastor encouraged me to get involved with another group, but I found their meetings to be more political posturing than fellowship.

In around 1984, I was introduced to the FCA. Right from the beginning, I found the FCA to be a marvelous mixture of "size matters" and "size doesn't matter." What I mean is, pastors of large "successful" churches were more than willing to spend time with guys like me who had big vision but no real clue how to obtain that vision.

At both local meetings and international conventions, giants the likes of Robert Forseth, Walter Pedersen, Warren Heckman and Paul Zettersten would freely share their encouragement with nobodies like me. Moreover, they often gave opportunity for us to learn and use our giftings. I was even allowed the dubious distinction of being the first to computerize the FCA, a fairly radical move in the mid-80s.

It is this willingness that's in our DNA — the more senior among us to help and make way for the more junior — that will continue to be the strength of the FCA into the future. It is one thing to pay to go to a seminar to hear some expert define his success, and it is quite another to learn success side-by-side with those "approved" (2 Corinthians 10:18).

–Dennis Hodulick, current FCA board member

My father was a FCA pastor for 60-plus years in the Midwest (Minnesota, Nebraska) and West Coast (Washington.) As a result, I was able to meet many wonderful pastors and missionaries with the FCA. Sometimes they would stay in our house. These were great men of God who impacted my life. On one occasion, we had Evangelist Dollarhyde for a week of meetings, and he stayed in our house. He was studying the Word in our living room when I snuck up on him with a bazooka gun (a toy gun that shot several rounds of plastic, ping pong ball size and weight). I started shooting these at him. He got up and chased me in fun. I realized at an early age that you can be serious about your Christian walk and the Word but still have fun.

FCA today is exciting to be a part of. It is particularly exciting for me to see churches and pastors not wanting the Pentecostal uniqueness to slip away into just a memory. People are urged to study the Word and to be filled with the Baptism of the Holy Spirit. Churches are being planted in houses and store-front buildings.

There are many creative ways that churches are using to build relationships with their community so that people will come to have a relationship with Jesus Christ. One such creative way is happening in Olympia, Washington,

Perspectives from Current Board Members

by Pastor Leanne, who is offering medical support for pets, as well as pet food to the homeless and low income in particular, thus building relationships with the community.

As Pastor Leanne served the people, she opened their hearts to hear about Jesus Christ. There is a great sense of cooperation between churches by supporting each other and by working together to evangelize and equip believers.

–Joe Finley, current FCA board member

Introduction
From the Author

Names of pastors, churches, conferences and dates are used extensively because they are linked together in the birthing, growth and development of the Fellowship of Christian Assemblies. They demonstrate the interaction, involvement and coast-to-coast exchange. Some dates and names seem to be in conflict, but without living historians or historical documentation, I have reported accounts as I have found them.

Much of the material and information contained in this book I've gleaned from a lifetime of being involved with the Independent Assemblies of God, now called the Fellowship of Christian Assemblies (FCA). As a child, our church (Friend Gospel Tabernacle, Friend, Nebraska) hosted a June convention almost every year. Our speakers came from surrounding states, but the main speakers were often E.C. Erickson, Duluth, Minnesota; Roy Johnson, Seattle, Washington; Clifford Johnson, Missionary from Liberia, West Africa; or A.M. Johnson, Brooklyn, New York. These men brought a big-city, big-church flavor, a worldwide missionary vision and outreach to our small-town, small-church, rural-village outlook.

My heart was stirred; I was deeply challenged to attend every service and serve in our local church 100 percent. While growing up, I was impacted and impregnated with

The History of the FCA

the Pentecostal teachings, evangelical full gospel doctrines and an emphasis on the autonomy of each local church.

After graduating from Bible college, my involvement in the FCA increased greatly. We traveled among the FCA churches throughout the Midwest for six months, holding "Kids' Krusades," speaking in youth camps, having revival services and filling in for pastors. We attended almost every Midwest convention, fellowship meeting, ministers' institute and Future of the Fellowship planning committee meetings, from then until the present. Beginning in 1960, it was my privilege to attend every annual national convention but three, a total of 47. Sources of information from conversations, sermons and papers presented have long since been lost, but I am indebted to those many, many people who shared their hearts and teachings on the FCA and especially on local church sovereignty and autonomy. Henry Jauhiainen has consistently shared FCA historical data, trivia, facts and teachings on the local church over the years. John Kennington taught repeatedly on the sovereignty of the local church.

In the beginning of our ministry as Bible college students, we were invited and urged to join a more organized Pentecostal group, far larger and worldwide in scope. Donna and I declined this generous offer in order to continue ministry within the FCA upon graduation. Throughout the first 10 or 15 years of full-time ministry, we were encouraged many times to consider joining a larger Pentecostal denomination because we would have a much better chance at advancing and acquiring a big

Introduction

church. My reaction was basically the same each time — I don't want a big church. I'm not ready for it, and I don't think I could handle it. Besides, if an organization helps in calling me to a bigger church, is God in it or is it political maneuvering? My roots were strongly entrenched within the FCA, their local church ecclesiology and the concept of interdependence while maintaining independence. I had been impacted by our annual June conventions and pastors from large city churches who came as guest speakers when I was young. So, our challenge: to grow a local church, but with the help of the Holy Spirit, not the help of an organization. Idealistic, I'm sure, but that was the manner of my mindset.

One
The Birth of a Movement

The Pentecostal/charismatic movement, as we know it today, traces its roots to the final years of the 1800s and early 1900s. It was birthed from among groups that taught a "Second Blessing," "Entire Sanctification" or "Baptism in the Holy Spirit" subsequent to salvation, all without speaking in tongues as a part of it. Most historical Pentecostal denominations were born from or influenced by these teachers. The "second experience" teaching set the stage for a later teaching, incorporating into this experience a baptism in the Holy Spirit that included speaking in tongues and other gifts of the Spirit. The FCA traces its early beginnings to these influences, teachings and preachers.

January 1, 1901 is often mentioned as the beginning of the modern classical Pentecostal outpouring. It was on this New Year's Day that Agnes Ozman first spoke in tongues in Charles F. Parham's Bible school in Topeka, Kansas. Others have claimed to receive this experience before 1900, but without similar documentation. Adherents and advocates were scorned, ridiculed and persecuted in the early years. In fact, for several decades, they were ignored or attacked as cultish, crude or a passing curiosity. It is true that many humble folk were attracted, including the poor, uneducated and alienated,

The History of the FCA

yet there were numerous leaders of intelligence, education and ability who were swept into the flow of the Holy Spirit. It was almost impossible to remain within your denomination if you accepted this Pentecostal teaching and a sure bet you'd be removed if you received the baptism of the Holy Spirit and spoke in tongues.

The charismatic movement, beginning in the late 1950s and early 1960s, slowly changed the outlook and attitude of many denominational people and leaders regarding the baptism in the Holy Spirit and this phenomenon of "glossolalia," or speaking in tongues. Suddenly people claimed to receive various gifts of the Holy Spirit, including tongues and healing. Times changed and church leaders often accommodated this formerly misunderstood teaching and experience. *Time* magazine, *Newsweek* and major newspapers reported "tongues" at Harvard University, Yale, Princeton, Notre Dame and other places. Father Dennis Bennett of St. Mark's Episcopal at Van Nuys, California, is often credited as the first to gain national attention for speaking in tongues. There seemed to be a spiritual hunger across the land as evidenced in the "Jesus People Movement." Again the media covered Pastor Chuck Smith of Calvary Chapel in California, who was baptizing thousands in the ocean. The Full Gospel Businessmen, led by Demos Shakarian, crossed all denominational lines.

No one could deny that large numbers of people were accepting and receiving this experience. Lutheran charismatics held annual Holy Spirit conferences in

One

Minneapolis, Minnesota, with record attendance gatherings of more than 10,000 people. Catholic charismatics gathered at Notre Dame with 30,000 to 40,000 people attending. To lose thousands of people would devastate most any denomination. They took a new approach, "don't ask, don't tell." Most denominations decided to quietly wait and see and allow charismatic movements to exist within their larger body of believers.

In the late 1980s, according to David B. Barrett, Ph.D., Cambridge University, writing in the *World Christian Encyclopedia*, 54,000 people per day were joining charismatic ranks or 19 million a year. Barrett says that the current Pentecostal/charismatic revival is the best reported and documented renewal movement in history.[1] With 372 to 400 million adherents, it is the second largest family in Christendom. He also states that all 10 of the largest churches in the world are Pentecostal/charismatic. And to think that there was none of this in 1900!

Research consultant for the Southern Baptist Convention and the Vatican, David B. Barrett, Ph.D., writes:

> These members are found in 11,000 Pentecostal denominations and in 3,000 independent charismatic denominations. Charismatics are now found across the entire spectrum of Christianity. They are found within all 150 traditional non-Pentecostal ecclesiastical confessions, families and traditions. Pentecostal/

charismatics (the generic term preferred here) are found in 8,000 ethno-linguistic cultures, speaking 7,000 languages, covering 95 percent of the world's total population. The sheer magnitude and diversity of the numbers involved boggle the imagination.[2]

Barrett predicted by 2000, there would be 619 million Pentecostal/charismatics worldwide, representing 29 percent of the world's Christians. Now, a decade later, we see how accurate his predictions were.

Dr. C. Peter Wagner, church growth specialist, Fuller Theological Seminary, wrote:

No other nonpolitical, non-militaristic human movement in history has grown as rapidly as the Pentecostal/charismatic movement has over the past 40 years. Even if some historian falsifies my hypotheses, my point in making it will remain; namely, that if this is contemporary work of the Holy Spirit, which I am fully convinced it is, Christian leaders are making a grievous error if they fail to lend an ear to what the Spirit is saying to the churches.[3]

By the end of the 20th century, newspapers and weekly news magazines were making their lists of the 100 most significant events. Just think, World War I, World War II,

One

airplanes — huge changes — and right in the middle was the Pentecostal/charismatic movement. Wow! How amazing is that?

Two
The Roots of the Pentecostal Movement

Let's go back to the humble beginning of the modern day outpouring. We trace our roots back to Methodism, John Wesley's theology of Christian perfection, the holiness movement and sanctification as a second definite work of grace. By 1901, foundational teaching was already in place among holiness preachers. They emphasized "Salvation, baptism in the Holy Spirit (without tongues), healing and the pre-millennial second coming. This would become classical Pentecostalism's four-fold doctrine."[4]

Liberals in Christianity emphasized the ethical and social aspects of religious life, typically meaning the natural tendencies to do and be good that are found in all people. By cultivating these virtues within us, this would bring them into full fruition. The holiness movement also emphasized the ethical, but from an exact opposite point of view. They insisted that there must be a supernatural work of the Holy Spirit to overcome the negative natural tendencies of human nature. Liberals spoke of an ongoing cultivation or Christian education to bring about these positive traits. The preachers and teachers of holiness and sanctification declared that only a dynamic work of the Holy Spirit could cleanse the heart of sin and change the old nature within.

Two

Within the holiness ranks there was a distinctive difference, however, from other evangelicals, fundamentalists, revivalists and evangelists. For in addition to the calling for decisions of repentance and faith in Christ unto salvation, the holiness preacher built on the dramatic conversion, with another call to experience the dynamic "second blessing." This was a supernatural sanctifying work of the Holy Spirit that freed one from sin's power. It was often a controversial teaching. The holiness movement and sanctification teaching brought the believer not into perfection but into a perfect love of God, a matter of motives.

The Methodist church became the cradle of the holiness movement in America, which grew out of the teachings of John Wesley. His theology provided the foundation for the birthing of the holiness teaching of the 19th century. He described "Christian Perfection" as a fundamental change in the motivational center of a person. Wesley believed that only a "willful transgression of a known law of God" should properly be called sin. Therefore, Christian perfection implied victory over all sin because the love of God purified and filled one's life. Wesley's emphasis on "holiness of heart and life" was readily received and embodied in the holiness movement which swept across American Christianity.[5]

In 1867, America saw the birth of the National Camp Meeting Association for the Promotion of Christian Holiness at Vineland, New Jersey, which soon spread beyond Methodism. In reality, this was the beginning of the modern holiness movement in the United States. As time went by, there were many breakaways from Methodism when people thought it was no longer really welcoming holiness. Numerous independent local churches sprung up, and many mini-denominations were birthed during these turbulent years. Larger groups were also started, such as the Wesleyan Methodists in 1843, then the Free Methodists in 1860, continuing on until the largest of these were the Church of the Nazarene, founded by Phineas F. Bresee in 1895, and the Pilgrim Holiness Church in 1922. Bresee's group and the Association of Pentecostal Churches in America, a group of holiness churches in the East, united in Chicago in 1907 to form the Pentecostal Church of the Nazarene. In 1919, the term Pentecostal was dropped due to its association with speaking in tongues, a practice not endorsed by the Church of the Nazarene.

Regional and national holiness associations cropped up, along with camps, magazines, schools and conferences. This mushrooming movement was more than mere reaction (to the liberals) but a genuine revival because people were spiritually hungry for God. They sought God in prayer meetings, conferences, studying the Word and camp meetings.

A paradigm shift had taken place. Casual Christianity and attending church occasionally was being replaced by an aggressive passion for God.

Now holiness and the experience of sanctification that had been emphasized beginning in the 1840s was gaining national attention following the Civil War.

In 1867, just after the war, the first national holiness camp meeting held in Vineland, New Jersey, became a turning point. This historic meeting called for a return to holiness living, but the call was couched in Pentecostal terms. People were invited to realize together a Pentecostal baptism of the Holy Ghost. This Pentecostal terminology was the result of a subtle shift that had been taking place among holiness teachers for several years.[6] For more than a century, Methodist teachers had spoken of sanctification and the baptism in the Holy Ghost as two sides of the same coin. Before the Civil War, most who received this experience called it their sanctification. Now, most referred to it as their baptism in the Holy Ghost (without speaking in tongues).

The term "Pentecostal" became the buzz word, the "in" word, to describe almost everything. In 1839, Asa Mahan, President of Oberlin College, published a book titled *Scripture Doctrine of Christian Perfection.* In 1870, he published a revision of the same book under the title *The Baptism of the Holy Ghost.* Pentecostal language was common in the holiness movement by 1900.

In 1897, the *Guide to Holiness* changed its subtitle from "and Revival Miscellany" to "and Pentecostal Life" because Pentecostalism was pervading Christian thought and aspirations more than ever before.[7]

Sermon series, books, women's groups, testimonies, camp meetings and choirs were described in some way by using the word Pentecostal.

The History of the FCA

How often we fail to see the hand of God at work! By using these scriptural terms, even though they didn't believe these things were for their generation, the holiness movement opened hearts and minds to the Biblical experience of the baptism with the Holy Spirit and speaking in tongues.

Three
Key Leaders

There were many leaders, but two played a significant part in what would evolve into the Pentecostal movement and teaching. They were Phoebe Worrall Palmer and Benjamin Hardin Irwin.

Palmer — Phoebe Worrall Palmer (1807-1874) was a Methodist, a lay revivalist, writer, feminist, humanitarian and editor. Her husband, Dr. Walter Palmer, was a physician. She was a leading personality in promoting the three states of spiritual life in the first half of the century: unconverted, converted and entirely sanctified. In 1839, the first periodical in America devoted exclusively to the holiness doctrine, *The Guide to Christian Perfection*, was published. It carried many of her articles, which insisted that entire sanctification is won not by spiritual struggle, but by trustfully claiming it as one of God's promises. Later the name was changed to *The Guide to Holiness*, and in 1865, the Palmers purchased the magazine. She, like many others, departed from Wesley by identifying the second moment of grace or second blessing, as it had come to be called, with the baptism of the Holy Spirit. She did not teach speaking in tongues as a part of it.[8]

The History of the FCA

Irwin — Benjamin Hardin Irwin was born in Missouri in 1854 and moved to Nebraska, where he practiced law and served as pastor of the Mount Zion Baptist Church. In 1891, as a lifelong Baptist, he came into contact with Wesleyan teaching. He claimed the entire sanctification experience and became a John Wesley Methodist. He fervently studied the teachings of Wesley on entire sanctification and became an ardent follower of John Fletcher, Wesley's co-worker, using his term, "the baptism of the Holy Spirit." He founded the Fire Baptized Holiness Movement in the late 1890s. He was elected president for life. He supposedly saw people baptized in the Holy Spirit and speaking in tongues before Parham in 1901 and Azusa in 1906. His ministry and influence were cut short, however, because he not only taught a first, second and third spiritual experience, he added a fourth, fifth and sixth. Then, in 1900, a written report of his ungodly lifestyle was published, and he dropped out of sight. [8]

There are many other lesser known leaders who traveled around speaking about this new phenomenon. In addition to the acknowledged holiness influence, we must note such diverse groups as Baptists, Congregationalists and Presbyterians who, with others of reformed non-Wesleyan theology, believed in sanctification. They differed in their concept of inbred sin as a permanent part of the human condition. For them, it is progressively subjugated, but this side of heaven's gate, it is never fully eradicated. And, following salvation, there is a second

Three

experience of grace that many of them called the baptism of the Holy Spirit. Their description of it was not primarily to purify the heart, but to empower the will to act, to witness, to sacrifice and to serve.[9]

During this mid- and late-19th century, many prominent leaders spoke and wrote concerning these issues. Among them were A.J. Gordon, A.B. Simpson, Charles Finney, Asa Mahan, R.A. Torrey, A.T. Pierson and Higher Life teachers of the English Keswick Movement. There was a receptive audience to teaching and writing about salvation, a second work/sanctification/baptism in the Holy Spirit, healing, the deeper life and the second coming of Christ.

Other leaders include:

Parham — Charles Parham (1873-1929) was the founder of the Apostolic Faith movement, which is still in existence, headquartered in Baxter Springs, Kansas. He suffered from poor health in his early years and after experiencing a dramatic healing, came to believe in divine healing. He began his career in the Methodist Episcopal church but left in 1895 to evangelize as an independent holiness preacher, teaching sanctification as a second work of grace, divine healing and the third experience of a baptism with the Holy Ghost and fire. According to some reports, he was influenced by Benjamin Hardin Irwin. He published a bi-monthly paper entitled *Apostolic Faith* and established the Bethel Healing Home in Topeka, Kansas.

Later, in 1900, he also established the Bethel Bible School near Topeka with about 40 students. He challenged the students to study the scriptures about the baptism in the Holy Spirit. Could they find consistent Biblical evidence for documenting a person receiving it? By December, they had concluded that the initial evidence of the baptism of the Holy Spirit was speaking in tongues, a conviction that became central in all of his subsequent teaching.

On January 1, 1901, a student named Agnes Ozman prayed for the experience and began to speak in tongues. Soon other students and Parham himself had received the baptism in the Holy Spirit with speaking in tongues. The impact seemed to wane until a revival broke out in Galena, Kansas, in 1903. Within seven years, his loosely organized Apostolic Faith Missions had spread throughout the lower Midwest with about 25,000 adherents. In 1905, he opened a Bible school in Houston, Texas, which served as a center for the movement. William Joseph Seymour, an African-American, arrived for training by Parham in his Bible college. He was not allowed in the classroom because he was a negro, so he sat out in the hall. He later became the apostle of the Azusa Street revival in Los Angeles. The Pentecostal movement that emerged in 1901 has spawned some 300 distinct American denominations.[10]

Seymour — William Joseph Seymour (1870-1922) accepted the invitation to minister at a black holiness mission in Los Angeles. He was rejected because he taught that the baptism in the Holy Spirit was always

Three

accompanied by speaking in tongues. He conducted cottage meetings, and on April 9, 1906, he and those present received the experience that he had preached about — they spoke in tongues. They soon had to move to a larger place to accommodate the crowds of seekers. They found it in a rundown building at 312 Azusa Street. Daily meetings attracted people from around the world. He is generally regarded as having effectively launched American Pentecostalism. He influenced William H. Durham, who in turn impacted many who became leaders of Pentecostal denominations of today, including the Fellowship of Christian Assemblies (formerly the Independent Assemblies of God).

Durham — William H. Durham (1873-1912), born in Kentucky, joined the Baptist church in 1891, but was not converted until 1898 in Minnesota. There he embraced the holiness teaching and soon entered the ministry, having experienced a vision of the crucified Christ. In 1901, he became pastor of a small mission in Chicago known as the North Avenue Mission. When people began receiving the baptism in the Holy Spirit, speaking in tongues and experiencing the gifts of healing, prophecy and such in his mission in 1906, he visited the Azusa Street Missions in Los Angeles. He received the baptism of the Holy Spirit and spoke in tongues on March 2, 1907. William Seymour prophesied that wherever Durham preached the Holy Spirit would fall upon the people.[11]

Durham's North Street Mission in Chicago became an

The History of the FCA

important center for his Pentecostal preaching and teaching. He was a dynamic leader, speaker and writer. He published a monthly magazine, *The Pentecostal Testimony*. The revival of Pentecost and tongues spread quickly throughout the land. He spoke strongly against the holiness teaching of an instantaneous sanctification, which he called the "Finished Work of Calvary." He is largely credited with developing the non-Wesleyan view of a progressive sanctification that many Pentecostal groups teach to this day. People thronged to his services, often staying into the wee hours of the morning. He reported in his magazine that it was not uncommon to hear people at all hours of the night speaking in tongues and singing in the Spirit. Thousands heard him preach, and all were gripped with the conviction that he was a "pulpit prodigy," as one writer put it. Durham and the North Street Mission became a leading center of International Pentecostalism. He died of pneumonia on July 7, 1912, at an early age while in Los Angeles.

What an ironic ending for a man who pioneered the teaching of the miraculous and supernatural.

Four
Durham and the FCA

Many consider William H. Durham as the great-great-grandfather of the Fellowship of Christian Assemblies. He taught that:

1. Conversion and sanctification were one act of God's justifying grace.
2. The benefits of Calvary are therefore appropriated for sanctification over the entire period of the Christian's life, rather than at a single moment after conversion.
3. Subsequent to salvation, the baptism in the Holy Spirit is immediately available to the believer because it is a part of the "Finished Work of Calvary," all a part of God's grace.
4. Speaking in tongues is the initial physical evidence of receiving this baptism in the Holy Spirit.

Durham is sometimes called the only original Pentecostal theologian.[12] Men and women who would become the founders and leaders of worldwide Pentecostal movements yet to be born soaked up his teaching and the Holy Spirit's moving in his early meetings in Chicago — great leaders who literally changed the course of history in numerous countries. A.H. Argue, E.N. Bell, Howard Gross, major players in the Assemblies of God, Daniel Berg (founder of the Assemblies of God in Brazil), Luigi Francescon (a pioneer of the Pentecostal movement in Italy), Aimee Semple-McPherson (who, prior to her marriage, was instantaneously healed of a broken ankle through Durham's ministry in 1910 and later became founder of the International Church the Foursquare Gospel), A.F. Johnson (an early leader of the FCA) and B.M. Johnson (another early leader of the FCA). Among those yet unknown were pioneers of the Assemblies of God, Pentecostal Assemblies of Canada, International Church of the Foursquare Gospel, plus others, and a number of Swedish Baptists, who would become founders of the Fellowship of Christian Assemblies (first known as the Independent Assemblies of God).[13]

Third, Durham was a strong proponent of local church autonomy and sovereignty. Many of the movements adopted a wide variety and combinations of types of church government. From the beginning, the Fellowship of Christian Assemblies' forefathers were deeply impacted and strongly stood for the same doctrine of ecclesiology as Durham taught. This was probably because many of them had been excommunicated from their denominations when they accepted the experience of the baptism of the Holy Spirit. They rightly concluded that no man should have the power to overrule Biblical truth. Durham would have been taught Congregationalism from his early years as a Baptist in Kentucky.

Four

He writes:

> [Organization] destroys the independent New Testament assembly life. It creates offices for men to fill, which exalts them above their brethren. It centralizes the government of the word of God, placing it in the hands of a few men and thus exalts them to positions of prominence; and, so far as we know, they have generally become puffed up and lost their spiritual power; or, if they do not become exalted, the people looked up to them entirely too much, and in many instances fairly worship them.[14]

Durham was severely criticized for his teaching on the finished work of Calvary, and one of the most outspoken was T.B. Barratt. He was a pastor in the Methodist Episcopal Church of Norway. Visiting the United States in 1906, he came into contact with the Pentecostal movement and went home an ardent proponent! He became the apostle of the European Pentecostal movement, founding many sovereign, indigenous, autonomous local churches throughout Europe, a magazine printed in many languages and the Filadelfia Church in Oslo, where he was the pastor until his death (1862-1940).

Five
Durham's Finished Work Controversy

Like many beginning movements, doctrinal diversity brought about a crisis of controversy. Durham's teaching on sanctification was a definite contradiction to many of the holiness teachings. Most of those in the holiness movement agreed with Wesley's position that a second instantaneous experience of "entire sanctification," or "Christian perfection," should follow conversion. Charles F. Parham and William J. Seymour were early members of the holiness movement. They and other leaders continued to believe the Wesleyan view. Now that they believed in a baptism in the Holy Spirit and speaking in tongues, it became a third work of grace. It would obviously follow one's sanctification or second work of grace experience. They generally concluded that there were three different experiences: conversion/justification, entire sanctification and the baptism in the Holy Spirit.

In 1910, Durham's teaching on the "Finished Work of Calvary" caused a significant stir. He taught that Christ finished the work on Calvary for the forgiveness of sins and for the sanctification of the believer. Regeneration positioned the believer to appropriate the benefits of sanctification, immediately and throughout his Christian walk. It was not an instantaneous experience, but a

Five

continual and progressive appropriation by faith. The teaching of instantaneous and entire sanctification would negate the need for an ongoing growth in sanctification during the believer's life, in Durham's way of thinking.

This crisis of controversy surfaced in 1910 when Durham shared them in a Chicago convention. He taught that there were only two, not three, spiritual experiences. He said sanctification was positionally complete at salvation, and that we are enabled to become more Christlike throughout our lives. Later he preached this doctrine at Malvern, Arkansas, in a camp meeting and convinced Howard Gross and many of Parham's former followers that the work was finished on Calvary. When Durham went to Los Angeles in February, he was not (yet) allowed to preach at Elmer K. Fisher's Upper Room Mission, a major center of the Pentecostal movement. In the absence of William Seymour, he preached at the Azusa Street Mission. The revival fires were rekindled, and it was known as the "second outpouring." When Seymour returned, however, he locked Durham out of his mission.

Durham continued preaching the "Finished Work of Calvary" message in Los Angeles with more than a thousand attending on Sundays and several hundred on weeknights. In a few months, he returned to Chicago. He wrote numerous articles and printed them in his paper, *The Pentecostal Testimony*. Parham and others thought his view to be diabolical and continued to oppose him. Long after Durham's death in 1912, his teachings continued to be divisive. When A.A. Boddy visited

California from England, it was said that he found the Pentecostal people in Los Angeles were just about tired of shaking their fists at one another.

The 1914 gathering in Hot Springs, Arkansas, was the beginning of the Assemblies of God denomination. Interestingly, they had no statement of faith as a basis of union, but the opening address by M.M. Pinson was entitled "The Finished Work of Calvary." It set the stage, and Durham's view of sanctification became the majority view among Pentecostals by the end of the next decade.[15]

This did not settle the controversy, but it cleared the air, establishing two distinctively different views. Each side began to learn to accept each other and live together. After World War II, there was enough cooperation to form the Pentecostal Fellowship of North America. The FCA was influenced by A.F. Johnson and B.M. Johnson, who were both filled with the Spirit and speaking in tongues at Durham's Chicago North Avenue Mission. Consequently, the FCA primarily accepted his teaching on the subject.

Six
Forefathers of the FCA

Another spiritual awakening, called the "New Movement," was taking place in Chicago among the Swedish Baptists. For about four years, members of Second Baptist Church met on Monday evenings to study the Spirit-filled life. They had an outbreak of the Holy Spirit in February of 1906. Among those attracted was Bengt Magnus Johnson, a graduate of the Divinity School of The University of Chicago, in the Swedish Department. Shortly after, B.M., as he was called, experienced the baptism in the Holy Spirit while visiting an Upper Peninsula church. Going back to Chicago, he was attracted to the meetings conducted by Durham at the North Street Mission, which were going full blast. He would later bring his strong Baptist stand on the autonomy and sovereignty of the local church with him into the Fellowship of Christian Assemblies (FCA). B.M. Johnson left the Baptists and became pastor of the Swedish Pentecostal Assembly in Chicago and in 1911 founded the Lakeview Gospel Church in Chicago, pastoring it for 25 years.

A.A. Holmgren, a Baptist minister, attended Durham's meetings in Chicago and received the baptism in the Holy Spirit. He ultimately went to Minneapolis to pastor the Philadelphia Pentecostal Church. He would go on to become a leader in the Scandinavian Assemblies of God and publish their periodical, *Sanningens Vittne*. John Feuk was also influenced by the New Movement and became the FCA pastor at Bloomington Temple in Minneapolis, along with John Moseid. Pethrus Swartz, another who was impacted, preached the Pentecostal message in his Baptist church for eight years and then later left the Baptists. He was the first pastor of the Homewood Full Gospel Church, then called West Auburn Park Baptist Church, founded in 1911 in Chicago, Illinois. Gunnar Wingren was so deeply moved that he sought God fervently. Sometime later he went to Brazil, where he pioneered the Pentecostal movement that changed the religious climate of the whole nation.

Seven
The Birthing of the Fellowship of Christian Assemblies (FCA)

On any given night there would be 25 to 30 pastors in Durham's meetings, listening, learning and leaving to take the message around the world. Another man who would be a major player in the beginning stages of the FCA was Arthur F. Johnson, who received the baptism in the Holy Spirit in Durham's mission in 1910. He served as chairman of the Scandinavian Assemblies of God for several years. A very vigorous and hardy young man, A.F. Johnson traveled and preached. After a time, he went to Duluth, Minnesota, and began having meetings. In time, he handpicked his protégée, E.C. Erickson, from Sister Bay, Wisconsin, to be pastor, which he did most successfully for more than 40 years. A.F. Johnson became mentor to Erickson in his early years.[16]

The *Herald of Pentecost* magazine, May 1953 issue, ran the following:

Rev. and Mrs. A.F. Johnson:
Four Decades of Ministry Together

Two faithful Pentecostal pioneers have marked the completion of forty years' united service to God and man.

The History of the FCA

Pastor and Mrs. Arthur F. Johnson, ministering in the Clarkfield (Minn.) Gospel Tabernacle, observed their four-decade wedding anniversary April 24 and looked back upon a path of Christian service that has taken them to many points in America and even a few European fields.

Pastor Johnson, who will soon be 65, was "born twice" in his native city, Chicago. He was converted to Christ as a teenager and "got into the Pentecostal revival" in the winter of 1907-8. Baptized in water at the old North Avenue Mission in Chicago that same year by Brother William Durham, he was in the Pentecostal movement to stay. Not long afterwards, Brother Johnson was filled with the Holy Spirit.

He launched out into evangelistic work in 1911, traveling with Brother C.M. Hanson. At Menominee, Michigan, up in the Upper Peninsula's lumber country, he met Mrs. Johnson, who had received the infilling of the Holy Spirit as a "Christmas gift" in 1909. They were married at Menominee in 1913.

The Johnsons did pioneer work in many Mid-Western communities and later pastured churches in Chicago, at various points in Minnesota and on the West Coast.

Over four years were spent in Europe. Their stay abroad included pioneer missionary work in the Baltic provinces, particularly Estonia in 1923. Here they saw many Estonians and Russians saved and filled with the Holy Spirit.

Their son, A. Philip, is pasturing Rock Church in Rockford, Illinois.

The Johnsons felt led to conclude their ministry in Clarkfield on their fortieth anniversary. They plan to return to Seattle, Washington, later this year, where for several years they have had their membership in Philadelphia Church.[17]

E.C. Erickson (1896-1980) was a Swedish-American evangelist, pastor, missions traveler, convention speaker and church planter. As a young boy, he grew up in Sister Bay, Wisconsin, attending the Swedish Baptist church with his family. In 1911, he, his family and a few others received the baptism in the Holy Spirit. After this Pentecostal experience, they, along with other members, left the church and began to conduct Pentecostal meetings in their homes. Deeply influenced by the autonomous local church principles of his early Baptist background, he remained forever convinced that it was the correct Biblical pattern for each and every local church to practice. Erickson was ordained as a minister with the Assemblies of God in 1918.[18]

Erickson and A.F. Johnson were the key leaders among a number of independent local churches in the upper Midwest. They had concentrated on English-speaking ministries, while maintaining contact with the two ethnic groups — the Scandinavian Independent Assemblies of God and the Scandinavian Assemblies of God. On an informal basis, Erickson and Johnson led the largest of the three groups, loosely known as the Independent Assemblies of God (now FCA). With their leadership, there was a greater acculturation into American life. Both were American born and fluent in English. They incorporated other nationalities, including A.C. Valdez of Hispanic extraction. Leading names included Aaron Peterson, John Mosied, Albert Mosied, John Feulk, Silas Miller, Gus Edwards, etc. Erickson noted about 12 key leaders who made up this primary group.[19]

The Scandinavian Independent Assemblies of God formed a corporation. There were strong feelings of local church autonomy and at the same time being incorporated nationally.

The Scandinavian Assemblies of God was the smallest of the three groups. They were primarily made up of folks who had just recently come from Sweden and were very loyal to the Swedish Pentecostal movement. From within their group arose those who pioneered the Philadelphia Church in Chicago.

Eight
The First Stage of the FCA
(1910 – 1950)

When the Assemblies of God, Springfield, Missouri, began organizing the North Central District of the Assemblies of God in 1922, Erickson strongly opposed it. He believed that the Scandinavian Pentecostal churches in the area should not join the organization. He had taught and preached that churches should remain autonomous and free from any denominational affiliation. Up until this time, those in the first group led by Erickson and Johnson had been ordained by the Assemblies of God. When the General Council of the Assemblies of God had been formed in 1914, it was primarily a ministers' fellowship. When they decided to further augment their structure and move up north to organize the North Central District, Erickson said, "We must draw the line."[20]

At age 26, Erickson called for a pastors' meeting in St. Paul, Minnesota, to discuss the possibility of establishing an informal fellowship of autonomous local churches. There was obviously a strong reaction against the formal organization being planned by the Assemblies of God. They would have a District Superintendent, area Presbyters and oversight over each local church and pastor. About 25 ministers from the three groups gathered to discuss the issue. Erickson reported that there was a unanimous desire and decision to be recognized as a fellowship of autonomous local churches. So, in 1922, in St. Paul, Minnesota, the three groups agreed to come under a common, informal banner — the Independent Assemblies of God, an unincorporated fellowship of local churches and ministers.[21]

In those early days, both E.C. Erickson and B.M. (Bengt Magnuson) Johnson were strongly opposed to written local church membership. B.M. violently so, but E.C., after visiting Sweden, changed his mind and instituted membership within his local church in Duluth. B.M. Johnson founded and pastored Lakeview Gospel Church in Chicago. Because of his strong stand against membership, a group broke away and began the Philadelphia Church in Chicago. In the days ahead, Philadelphia Church was pastored by Joseph Mattsson (Boze). He became the link to the Fellowship in Chicago, while, for a time, the Lakeview Gospel Church became a lesser link.

In 1935, the Scandinavian Assemblies of God dissolved their corporation and declared themselves totally a part of the non-incorporated group known as the Independent Assemblies of God (now known as the Fellowship of Christian Assemblies). Their big thrust was local church autonomy and congregational life or, put another way, Christ's Lordship and the working of the Holy Spirit's power. In this 1935 conference, they declared their opposition to any permanent organization with articles of faith and bylaws. Interestingly, they knew what they didn't

Eight

want, but weren't so sure what they did want. For many years, they would probe the limits of cooperation among local churches without losing autonomy.[22]

Each local church emphasized the Lordship of Jesus Christ. He was head of the church, not an organization or elected official from the outside. Therefore, each local church was sovereign and autonomous to interpret scripture and obey it. Two ordinances were observed — water baptism by immersion following conversion and the Lord's supper/communion. The offices of pastor(s), elder(s) and deacon(s) were recognized, as well as the participation of people in worship and government of the local church. The direction was clear. The emphasis was more on what they were going to say together than what they were going to do together. They would be orators, not organizers (Henry Jauhiainen).

At the 1935 conference, there were 54 pastors and evangelists present and 21 missionaries. Among them were the first Canadians, Rev. and Mrs. C.O. Nordin, Amisk, Alberta. Erickson returned home and launched the magazine, *Herald of Faith,* in January of 1936, at 39 years of age.

In the January 1936, Volume One, Number One issue of *Herald of Faith*, we gain insights into the growing identification and expression of the Independent Assemblies of God. On the front cover is the stated purpose: "Published in the interests of full gospel faith and fellowship." (Subscription price, $1.00 per year, Editor, E.C. Erickson, 1515 West Superior Street, Duluth,

The History of the FCA

Minnesota.) The very first article by Erickson is "The Beginning of Months." He drew from Exodus 12:2, 3, 11, 37 and started with the text, "This month shall be unto you the beginning of months. It shall be the first month of the year unto you."

On page 3 the caption "IMPORTANT NOTICE" reads:

> *The Herald of Faith* is a newcomer in the field of Full Gospel literature. Time only will tell if it has a place to fill in that field. Our first thought concerning a publication was a local church paper serving primarily the interests of our work in Duluth; but after our intentions became known, many requests came in urging us to make it a monthly publication serving also the interests of other Independent Assemblies.[23]

Erickson continued by saying that he felt ill-equipped and already overburdened with work, but the need was great for a publication among our Independent churches. If there was a good response, cooperation and support for this new venture, they would try to continue it with God's help.

It contained newsy updates on the ministry of six local churches in the upper Midwest; the missionary work in Liberia, West Africa, being conducted by Rev. and Mrs. C.F. Walin and the Clifford Johnsons; and the missions work in Korea by Gladys Parsons and Elfreda Ofstead.

Eight

Only eight pages in all, it included more church news on the back page, where it also announced the results of the convention in Minneapolis, Minnesota, at Bloomington Temple on October 6-13, 1935. At their annual meeting, the ministers of the Scandinavian Assemblies of God unanimously resolved to join forces with the Independent Assemblies.

According to the article, a motion was made and carried that they "elect a traffic secretary to make up the list of the united ministers to be sent to the Transportation bureaus. Brothers A.A. Holmgren, B.M. Johnson and A.F. Johnson were nominated."

And finally, two forthcoming conventions were advertised: Tenth Anniversary Service, Philadelphia Church, Chicago, Illinois, March 14-15, 1936, Joseph Mattsson (Boze), pastor; and a Three-Day Convention, Glad Tidings Tabernacle, Oshkosh, Wisconsin, March 24-26, 1936, J.E. Robinson, pastor. Letters poured in praising this new ministry in print, and Erickson kept producing it.

After Nordin returned to Canada, he spent a lifetime preaching, teaching and ministering among the Canadian Fellowship churches. Five years after the 1935 convention, the ranks had grown to 160 pastors numbered among the Independent Assemblies of God.

Nine
Conferences

Annual conferences became the glue that bonded the Fellowship of Christian Assemblies, pastors, evangelists and missionaries together. Unlike many other groups, it was not denominational/organizational membership, an exacting doctrinal expression of faith and practice or even common foreign missions and church planting projects that yoked them to one another. They came together out of a pure desire for fellowship, the love of the brethren, spiritual hunger for the Word and the commonality of belonging to autonomous local churches. They gathered annually for their national conference, but they also came together regularly in regional conferences lasting two to five days in churches large and small, plus single-day fellowship gatherings. Some of the meetings were well planned and thought out; others simply convened and whomever showed up shared in preaching and teaching. There was no involuntary involvement. In the first year (1936), *Herald of Faith* magazine advertised forthcoming conventions more than 20 times.

They emphasized exposition, inspiration and encouragement, not business meeting agendas, elections, denominational demands and duties. There were no elected officials, offices or positions. Playing politics was nil because there was nothing to run for or against or

Nine

achieve that would give power, prestige or position. All stood equal at the foot of the cross.

The first national convention of this new group was held in Brooklyn, New York, May 26-31, 1936, at the Salem Pentecostal Assembly, hosted by Pastor Arne Dahl. The convention was publicized in the April and May 1936 editions of the *Herald of Faith*. The advertised speakers were Pastors E.C. Erickson, Duluth, Minnesota; Joseph Mattsson (Boze), Chicago, Illinois; and Evangelist Helen Jepson, Minneapolis, Minnesota.

For several years, annual national conferences alternated between Duluth, Minnesota, and Chicago, Illinois. Open forums were a common feature. In the first daytime conference session, the ministers were asked what topics they wanted discussed. Then there was a simple show of hands to determine which ones were of greatest interest. They might choose one or several. Topics were prioritized according to interest, and the floor was open for anyone to address the topic of the moment. Usually a moderator was chosen and time limits set for each speaker.

Lively, spirited debate usually followed until the cooks called that the meal was ready. Pastors, young and old, could share their views, air their opinions and ask their questions. Sometimes lay people joined in on the discussions. Regular topics of interest included the various aspects of local church autonomy, the baptism in the Holy Spirit, tongues and the other gifts, differing views of the end times, practical holiness and interaction of local churches in world missions. Current themes and trends were usually hot topics as well.[24]

Herald of Faith magazine was later published in Chicago from the Philadelphia Church. The May 1942 issue lists Lewi Pethrus as Editor and E.C. Erickson as Consulting Editor. It was still $1.00 per year. It contained articles by Pethrus, Erickson, A. Philip Johnson, Joseph Mattsson (Boze), Henry Carlson and Einar Waermo. The magazine continued to feature missionary reports, along with news from local churches and advertisements of conventions.

Two news reports are noteworthy: Salem Pentecostal Assembly's 15th anniversary conference, Brooklyn, New York, hosted by Pastor A.W. Rasmussen. This was a change of venue for the convention; it wasn't going to be in Duluth or Chicago this year. Secondly, the Easter Sunday arrival in Chicago of Lewi Pethrus from Sweden to pastor the Philadelphia Church was very momentous. He was leaving the largest Pentecostal church in the world during a World War crisis to come to a fledgling new Scandinavian church in Chicago.

Ten
FCA Philosophy

The basic operating philosophy of the Fellowship was now in place, and it would continue on up to about 1950: The FCA opposed organization and church government beyond the local church, it loved conferences and conventions, where preaching and fellowship abounded, and it strongly emphasized missions. The local church hosted these gatherings and planned these events. Later pastors added business sessions at the annual conferences to decide the location of the next conference, and planning committees were elected two years in advance to select themes, topics and assign speakers. In years to come, conventions would often be held in a hotel convention center. During these early years, 1910 through1950, with little or no organization, the Fellowship of Christian Assemblies, known then as the Independent Assemblies of God, enjoyed harmony, growth and fruitfulness.[25]

Common characteristics of this period include:

1. Interchurch leadership rested upon key pastors by a sort of informal consensus. They were often located in key churches in metro areas such as Brooklyn, New York; Chicago, Illinois; Minneapolis and St. Paul, Minnesota; Tacoma,

Washington; Seattle, Washington; and Duluth, Minnesota, plus other churches in the area.

2. Leadership pastors were seen as natural leaders, not through elections to office, but through gifting by God and spiritual insight, character and accomplishment.

3. They were able to articulate what they felt God was saying and doing and what God wanted them to be saying and doing.

It was natural that many simply followed, acknowledging lesser leaders following greater leaders as right. This all seemed very scriptural, natural and it was also very Scandinavian. Lewi Pethrus (1884-1974), pastor of the world-renown Filadelfia Church, Stockholm, Sweden, influenced the American Fellowship immensely. He had begun visiting the USA churches in the mid-20s, and his writings and publications were well read. The Fellowship looked more and more to Pethrus as a long-distance mentor. It must have been very reassuring to these few FCA pastors to have this humble leader, who pastored the largest Pentecostal church in the world for 40 years, mentor them. He often spoke at their conventions without mentioning his own church, its size or growth. He spoke of the quality of church life, evangelism, conversion, membership, water baptism, baptism in the Holy Spirit, church discipline and local church autonomy.

Pethrus was also a world-renown figure beyond the Pentecostal movement. He was recognized for his holistic

Ten

vision for the Christian life and the moderation, dignity and realism of his expectations of spiritual development. He founded the Filadelfia Church Rescue Mission, the Filadelfia Publishing House, the Filadelfia Bible School, the periodical *Evangelii Harold*, a secondary school, a national daily newspaper, a savings bank and a worldwide radio network (I.B.R.A.).

Pethrus had become a Pentecostal in 1907 when attracted to the revival in Oslo, Norway. He was influenced by T.B. Barratt, a prominent Pentecostal pastor in Oslo. His many books and articles were translated into numerous languages and influenced the Pentecostal world at large.[26]

Eleven
Reaction Era of the FCA
(1950s – 1980s)

Reaction Against Denominations

A second stage or period of the FCA, the 1950s through the 1980s, might be called the Reaction Era.

First and foremost was the reaction to any kind of church organization beyond the local church. The Assemblies of God were always close to their line of fire. The FCA's early name, Independent Assemblies of God, carried that feeling of reaction to the larger group that had been organized in a combination of Congregational, Presbyterian and partially Episcopalian-type governments. Through the years, numerous FCA pastors and local churches had joined the Assemblies of God, always a sore spot with the FCA.

Reaction against organization was heightened through a curious incident. Because of a unique mailing error out of the Minneapolis District Office of the Assemblies of God, a letter fell into the hands of E.C. Erickson. It outlined a plan for taking over one of the FCA churches in northern Minnesota. E.C., known as one who never backed off from a good fight, jumped into his car and drove all the way from Duluth to Minneapolis to face his adversarial brother. After that incident, he made sure the

Eleven

Fellowship never forgot Two Harbors, Minnesota, which had been another Fellowship church lost to the Assemblies of God with documented strategy for its overthrow. This had been something suspected in the past by FCA pastors, but without evidence until that time. No thought was given, however, to organizing the FCA in response to the ongoing slippage of churches into other organized groups. In fact, on the contrary, local autonomy was advocated more strongly and denominational organization spoken against more vehemently. Had the FCA appointed or elected regional leaders to step in and help churches in transition or crisis, it would have kept them from joining other groups.

Communication in the FCA was always at its best while in conference, but in between these meetings there lacked good networking to handle situations. A craving arose for something to meet this need. G.K. Flockstra, an associate pastor to E.C. Erickson for many years, tried to bring the Baptist Association idea into the FCA. Privately people patted him on the back and encouraged him to proceed, but publicly in conventions they backed away, giving him no support. They recognized the need, felt the loneliness of pastoring and facing decisions singularly, but were not willing to risk *the wrath of the powers that be* to identify with such an idea publicly in a convention. Many witnessed local churches that floundered by themselves without knowing who to turn to for direction, help, leadership, counsel and when seeking potential pastors when their pastors moved on to another church. Small wonder so many turned to nearby Pentecostal organizations and district officials who not only helped, but hugged, them right into their denomination.

Discouraged, Flockstra left the FCA and joined another group, leaving the need unmet and a continuing stream of pastors and churches finding the needed network in more organized groups.[27] This only increased the antagonism between the FCA and other denominations. In reading the early editions of *Herald of Faith* and *Herald of Pentecost*, it is striking how many churches that were a part of the FCA are no longer with the FCA.

Reaction Against Ministry Education Apart from the Local Church

In addition, the FCA pastors reacted to any sort of formal preparation for ministry, such as seminary training, whether for pastoral, missionary, evangelist or local church lay leader.

FCA members expected a person to become active in their local church, coming up through the ranks from a rookie learner to a responsible leader. In the larger churches, it worked quite well because there were multiple ministries led by accomplished laity who could mentor the newcomer. The pastor's teaching ministry often was solid exposition of scripture three or more times a week, plus numerous guest speakers of renown who conducted series of one or two weeks of special services. Such training often

Eleven

surpassed what might be received in a Bible school or seminary.

But this was true in only a few of the larger churches. It is possible leading pastors preached against going away for ministerial preparation out of reaction to some schools that had become modernistic and because some students left and never returned, joining other groups. At this time the FCA had no Bible schools. And some may have felt slighted by those who chose to go away for training. Hence, they advocated local church training, mentoring and preparation for the ministry.

Later on after World War II, as people came home with educational benefits from military service, they began shipping out to Bible colleges and seminaries. Henry Jauhiainen was probably the first from the Fellowship to attend a seminary. Following a Scandinavian idea, short-term Bible schools were held in Brooklyn, New York, Chicago, Illinois, and Duluth, Minnesota. It was an uncertain time, and therefore it created conflict between some pastors and their parishioners.

In time, most would choose going to school and, in fact, the FCA would eventually start several schools of its own. But FCA leadership always encouraged and implemented local church training and involvement.

Reaction Against Para-Church Ministries

A third reaction could surely have been predicted. It was the feeling the FCA developed toward para-church ministries and organizations. Because it was outspoken about local church principles of autonomy and opposed to organization beyond that, there was bound to be a basic rejection of anyone or anything not related to and under the authority of a local church. Besides surfacing in their reaction to ministerial training schools, it also showed up toward para-church missions organizations and missionaries, college campus groups, evangelistic associations, healing ministries organizations, Youth for Christ and other similar groups.

Perhaps more than a little pride was involved: "If it isn't us, it isn't good." The teaching and thinking, however, were Biblical. Christ established the church, not some other kind of organization. Members of the FCA were staunch believers in their local church; they attended and worshipped there, served, gave, ministered and grew spiritually in and through the local church. They felt strongly that the church must be set in order Biblically with pastor(s), elders and deacons. It must function with integrity, accountability and credibility. People must live holy lives according to scripture in order to be leaders. In para-church organizations, these truths might be overlooked, circumvented or ignored.

Anti-Indifference

A fourth reaction was to the plight of the lost at home and abroad. Foreign missions were coordinated primarily through the key churches and pastors. For example, the

Eleven

Duluth Gospel Tabernacle pioneered missions in Liberia, West Africa. Many other churches and pastors rallied around this outreach and sent money, coordinated prospective missionaries and added these things to their prayer emphasis. *Herald of Faith* magazine became an additional vehicle for missions reporting and therefore giving. After being started in Duluth, Minnesota, by E.C. Erickson, and published there, this heavy burden was later transferred to Pastor Joseph Mattsson (Boze) at the Philadelphia Church in Chicago. Although Mattsson and Erickson were totally different in personality, they shared many similar convictions regarding local church autonomy, ministry and missionary outreach.

Evangelistic outreach took place in different ways in different places. In Chicago in the early 1940s, the Philadelphia Church was in the midst of a massive Scandinavian population immigration. They extended a call to Lewi Pethrus in 1940 to come from Sweden to the United States to pastor the church and probably try to reap the harvest spiritually. He agreed to come for three years. Political red tape because of World War II kept his family from joining him. For that, and possibly unstated reasons, he stayed only six months before returning to Sweden.

While Chicago was putting their energy into evangelizing immigrant Scandinavians, Duluth had no such influx of immigrants. They had to minister more widely and thus became a very strong home missions church. They founded churches from northern Michigan across northern Wisconsin and northern Minnesota and eventually all the way to Los Angeles.

Missionary outreach was a vital part of the FCA from its beginning years of ministry.

Twelve
Additional Insights from Early FCA Churches

Bloomington Temple

Bloomington Temple, Minneapolis, Minnesota, had become a significant church under the leadership of John Fuek and John Moseid. It was a strong church that originated from the Franklin Street Mission. Erickson recalls it as the strongest Pentecostal church in the Twin Cities. When asked why it declined and ultimately died, he shared his personal opinion that when Charles Price, the healing evangelist, came to town, Pastors Fuek and Moseid took a stand against him. Other churches reaped a bountiful harvest, while theirs began a decline. When Price came to Duluth, holding meetings in the ice arena for two to three months, Pastor Erickson cooperated and reaped a large harvest.[28]

It was in Duluth that Pastor W.H. Sproule of Madison, Wisconsin, attended the Charles S. Price meetings and became interested in the baptism in the Holy Spirit in about 1927. He was filled with the Holy Spirit and spoke in tongues. He led the Madison Gospel Tabernacle congregation (now Lake City Church) into accepting both the truth and the experience of the Spirit-filled life, thus becoming the first Pentecostal church in Madison.

The History of the FCA

Salem Gospel Temple

Salem Gospel Tabernacle, Brooklyn, New York, was founded in 1926 and led first by Pastor Arne Dahl, second by A.W. Rasmussen, third by Harry Ring, fourth by Arthur M. Johnson and then by Arne Dahl. It grew to become a key church in the Northeast and a lead church in the Fellowship. It helped start numerous branch churches, became heavily involved in world missions, Fellowship activities and conventions and produced many pastors who went forth to serve God in the ministry. The following article titled "Salem Gospel Tabernacle Celebrates 30th Anniversary" appeared in the March 1956 issue of *Herald of Pentecost.*

On March 26, 1926, 24 people came together in a rented hall at 5111 5th Avenue, Brooklyn, New York. The Pentecostal revival had come to the area in 1907. The purpose of forming this new assembly was the growing conviction that the work of God would not succeed and go forth the way God had promised it to do unless assembly life was conformed to the apostolic and New Testament pattern concerning church government, church discipline, etc. Strife and lack of unity concerning assembly order according to the revealed will of God in His word, hindered and hampered the work of God, we are sorry to say, in the old Pentecostal circles.

Twelve

Note: The name of the church was changed several times over the years. They planted a church in New Hyde Park, which continued until 2010. Another was on Long Island at Smithtown. It has become a leading FCA church of 2,000 to 2,500 people presently pastored by Gary Zarlengo. Pastors Wesley Braaten, Lloyd Jacobsen and Walter Pederson all came out of Salem Gospel Tabernacle. They have been strong leaders in the FCA.[29]

Duluth Gospel Tabernacle – Duluth, Minnesota

Duluth Gospel Tabernacle was founded and incorporated by A.F. Johnson in 1916 and turned over to E.C. Erickson two years later in 1918. It had its earliest beginnings in 1908, however, when Mrs. Jamison, wife of a Presbyterian minister in Duluth, received the baptism in the Holy Spirit. Various preachers and teachers conducted meetings in those early years, endeavoring to get a mission church started, but without success. A.F. Johnson arrived in Duluth in 1916 and gathered together the scattered Pentecostal remnants. Although he was a traveling evangelist, he did not abandon this little flock until a church was formed and a pastor in place. Erickson pastored there for 46 years and continued 12 more years as pastor emeritus.[30]

E.C. Erickson was ahead of his peers in Americanizing the work and ministry. He was very ecumenical. For a number of years, he had strong opposition to the

The History of the FCA

Assemblies of God leadership and organization, but later entered into a close, loving relationship with its leaders. He traveled a lot in the field throughout the Fellowship after he was released from pastoring by his church. He was deeply involved in evangelism, church planting and world missions. He attended conferences faithfully, spoke extensively and hosted a summer convention annually.

His ministry and leadership probably impacted the FCA during these years more than anyone else's. The Duluth Gospel Tabernacle seated 1,000 people and was regularly filled. He was theologically balanced. For many years, he was influenced by a Baptist pastor from Toronto, T.T. Shield. He received two sermons a week from him. It influenced his sermon style and line of thought. He found Roy Johnson in upper Michigan and liked him. He brought him into the FCA and later introduced him to the Ballard Pentecostal Church in Seattle, Washington, where Albert Moseid was pastor from 1939 to 1947.

Philadelphia Church – Seattle, Washington

In the 1940s, Roy Johnson was called to pastor the Ballard Pentecostal Church in Seattle. He began a whole new era in the Pacific Northwest, where he pastored for 30 years (1947-1977). The church's name was changed to the Philadelphia Church and became a leader in size and scope. Johnson led the church into ever-increasing involvement with and giving of hundreds of thousands of dollars to missions. Attendance grew to more than 1,200, while helping birth some two dozen new churches in the Northwest.

Saturday night prayer meetings became a mainstay. A local church Bible school (Seattle Bible College) was birthed in 1955 that grew to serve the whole Fellowship. Dozens of young people were trained and thrust into full-time ministry from the Philadelphia Church. Consistent evangelistic outreach took place, and cooperative tent meetings and strong preaching attracted hundreds of people.

It became a model that many looked to as an example of a strong New Testament Pentecostal autonomous local church. Johnson's ministry and leadership influenced all of the FCA throughout the United States, Canada and missions worldwide.

Homewood Full Gospel Church – Chicago, Illinois

In Chicago, the West Auburn Park Swedish Baptist Church was formed in the early 1900s. In 1922, when it became an Independent Full Gospel Church, "Swedish" and "Baptist" were dropped from its name. Later it became Beulah Temple and was pastored by Jack Whitesell from 1953 to 1964. Later, it became Homewood Full Gospel Church, growing under the leadership of Pastor Walter Pederson to more than 2,000 people during the 1970s and 1980s. Reverend George Thomas became the next pastor and served there until 2007.

The History of the FCA

The name was changed to All Nations Community Church, and it continued to be a key church in the Fellowship at that time.

Thirteen
FCA in Canada

A parallel movement, the Fellowship of Christian Assemblies in Canada, had its origins in the western provinces, particularly in Alberta. One of its significant pioneers, C.O. Nordin, served from 1916 to 1957 and was the first Canadian participant in early U.S. conferences of the Fellowship. In 1945, Rev. and Mrs. Thomas E. Crane joined with Rev. and Mrs. A.W. Rasmussen in founding Edmonton Gospel Temple and Temple Bible College, located in Edmonton, Alberta, Canada. Crane became principal of the college, as well as associate pastor in the church.

The venerable Arthur F. Johnson never held a large church pastorate. Yet, he was a bellwether in the FCA and had a ministry that influenced many pastors and churches. Lewi Pethrus continued to influence the FCA after returning to Sweden, both in return visits and through his books and articles.

Fourteen
The Latter Rain Teaching
Causes Controversy in the Church

Another major concern that deeply divided and split the FCA was the "Latter Rain Movement" coming out of the Sharon Bible Institute, North Battleford, Saskatchewan, Canada, in 1947. Regardless of its early origins, it eventually became extremely controversial. The form of worship and prophetic claims produced negative reactions from many Pentecostal groups. Among the teachings that were controversial:

1. Gifts of the Spirit were distributed by the laying on of hands.
2. Certain people were invested with the ministry of Apostle.
3. Apostles held immense power to interpret scripture, make decisions, etc.
4. A great deal of guidance came through personal prophecy.

The FCA took a cautious view for a while. Some churches went with the flow of the Latter Rain, especially Philadelphia Church, Chicago, Illinois, pastored by Joseph Mattsson (Boze). In 1949, a showdown was imminent at the convention held in Chicago. Lewi Pethrus came from

Fourteen

Sweden, urging the FCA to buy the whole field, to get the treasure. Erickson from Duluth spoke against the excesses and unscriptural experiences and teachings as he saw them. A.W. Rasmussen and Joseph Mattsson (Boze) both spoke for the Latter Rain. Erickson prophesied to Pethrus: "When this movement, as we have seen it here, arrives in Sweden, you will be the first man to shut the door on it." It was accurately fulfilled. A majority of the FCA (then Independent Assemblies of God) pastors stood with Erickson.[31]

A couple of years later, in 1951, in a conference in Los Angeles, the rift was irreversible, and we had two groups. A.W. Rasmussen formed an incorporated group that was called the Independent Assemblies of God International and was headquartered in San Diego, California. We remained the Independent Assemblies of God (of which I am a member), not incorporated, an informal group of autonomous churches and pastors now known as the Fellowship of Christian Assemblies.

With the split into two groups, the Independent Assemblies of God (now Fellowship of Christian Assemblies) lost their monthly magazine, *Herald of Faith*. But by that summer of 1951, a new one was born, *Herald of Pentecost*.

The September 1951, Volume I, No. 2 issue featured the lead article highlighting the National Convention, October 2-7, at Immanuel Christian Assembly, Los Angeles, California, hosted by Pastor Paul Zettersten. This church was started by E.C. Erickson and the Duluth

The History of the FCA

Gospel Tabernacle. The guest speaker was Donald Gee from England. Ted Lanes of Duluth, Minnesota, was the editor of *Herald of Pentecost*, and Rockford, Illinois, was the office address. The byline stated: "Published by the National Publications Committee as the voice of Independent Pentecostal Churches." The same format was being followed — inspirational articles, missionaries' reports, news of local churches and advertisements of conventions and Fellowship meetings.

Early in the new year (February 1951), *Herald of Pentecost* was administered by a new editor, Henry Jauhiainen, who had become assistant pastor at the Duluth Gospel Tabernacle under senior pastor E.C. Erickson. The printed page continued to play a major role among the churches. A. Philip Johnson, Rockford, Illinois, pastor of Rock Church, was in charge of circulation and subscriptions. The Publications Committee was made up of pastors: Harry Ring (Brooklyn, New York), Paul Zettersten (Los Angeles, California), Roy Johnson (Seattle, Washington), A. Philip Johnson (Rockford, Illinois) and E.C. Erickson (Duluth, Minnesota), with Henry Jauhiainen, Editor.

Years later, in the 1960s, when Rev. Robert Anderson became pastor of the Philadelphia Church in Chicago, the rift there was healed and fellowship restored as they again became active in the FCA. Crane later pastored the Madison Gospel Tabernacle (now Lake City Church), Madison, Wisconsin, during the 1950s and drew it back into the Fellowship. In 1961, the Cranes returned to pastor

Fourteen

the Edmonton Gospel Temple and to reopen the Temple Bible College, which had been closed for two years, bringing about reconciliation between the church and the FCA.

The turmoil generated by the "Latter Rain Movement" stimulated a quest for clearer identity and more cohesive, practical cooperation within the FCA.

Fifteen
Bible Training Schools

The Philadelphia Church, Chicago, Illinois, began holding annual Bible teaching sessions in the late 1940s. The following was a full-page advertisement in the August 1946 *Herald of Faith* magazine:

WHY DOES THE CHRISTIAN CHURCH
HAVE SO LITTLE SUCCESS?

- The secret of success
- How to attain the goal
- Many other timely subjects

You will find the answers to these questions during the Bible sessions at the annual 1946 Bible Course in Chicago — one full month (October), five hours Bible study daily — for pastors, evangelists, missionaries, elders, deacons, Sunday school teachers and other friends who feel the need of a time of rest under the influence of the rightly divided word of God.

Teachers: Rev. John W. Follette, New Paltz, New York; Pastor Lewi Pethrus, Philadelphia Church, Stockholm, Sweden; plus others

Fifteen

For information, write: Bible Course, c/o Philadelphia Church, 5317 North Clark Street, Chicago 40, Illinois.[32]

As other churches began sending their people to study the Bible, a local church Bible school was born. The school was lengthened to two semesters and then in 1950, offered full-time classes.

In the 1950s and 1960s, Jack Whitesell shared his teaching ministry at Chicago Bible College (CBC). In 1954, a four-year program was instituted, and the CBC was up and running with Dr. Russell Meade as president. In 1956, CBC became separate from the church in identity, location and administration. In 1976, Dr. Meade passed away and many changes took place. Pastor Robert Anderson became president.

In 1977, CBC left the inner city to share the classroom facilities of Christian Assembly in Mt. Prospect, Illinois, a Chicago suburb, at the invitation of Pastor Daryl Merrill, also vice president and academic dean of CBC. In 1981, each made name changes — to Christian Life Church and Christian Life College. Shortly afterwards, Dr. Daryl Merrill was named president of CLC.

The Seattle Bible Training School (now Seattle Bible College) was founded in 1955 by Roy Johnson, pastor of Philadelphia Church, Seattle, for the training and preparation of ministers, missionaries and Christian workers. Soon graduates were serving as pastors in Fellowship churches as associates and as missionaries around the world. SBC continues to train, equip and mobilize men and women for ministry.

Faithful teachers came from near and far. Prominent leaders over the years were: Dr. Arthur Petrie, Rev. E.C. Erickson, Rev. Ern Baxter, Rev. Roy Johnson, Rev. John Egerdahl, Mrs. Joy Scheilz, Rev. Gwilym Frances, Rev. Gunnar Jacobsen, Mrs. Evelyn Welk, Rev. H.E. Collingridge, Rev. Samuel T. Smith and Rev. Paul Cornish. Currently, key leaders are Dan Fick, Bryan Johnson and Rev. Paul Zettersten (1994).

Also, Temple Bible College, Edmonton, Alberta, Canada, mentioned earlier, was led by T.E. Crane.

Sixteen
Struggling Fellowship Magazines and Broadening the Support Base

A monthly magazine was very important to these scattered independent local churches. There were no area bishops, sectional superintendents or appointed/elected leaders at the top. Nor was there a national organization. Local fellowship meetings, regional conferences and the annual national conventions brought them together for great preaching, teaching, open forums, friendships and inspiration. It was, however, the monthly magazine that kept everyone informed of local church activity, accomplishments, world missions outreaches and announced where and when the next conference would be.

Keeping a magazine going, getting it published each month and maintaining it financially in the black was an awesome, tremendous task. Some issues became two months in one. Appeals were made for additional subscriptions to increase the income. The local church that carried the burden of printing it often received negative comments with little positive support. The first magazine, *Herald of Faith*, was left to the breakaway group called the Independent Assemblies of God International in 1951. This was a result of the "Latter Rain" split in the Independent Assemblies of God, now called the FCA.

The History of the FCA

These in-between years were supplemented with mimeographed newsletters and ministry updates but did not have the same effect. For several years, it was a constant concern and an ongoing topic for discussion at conferences. All seemed in favor of once again publishing a monthly Fellowship magazine, but how could it be accomplished? Who could do it? How could it be financed? What would keep it from being unduly influenced by one church, one pastor, one point of view?

In 1951, a new magazine, the *Herald of Pentecost* was birthed by Erickson and Jauhiainen in Duluth, Minnesota, published by the Duluth Gospel Tabernacle. Yet, in only four years, the October/November 1956 issue of *Herald of Pentecost* had a front page headline article that read: "We trust this will be a temporary suspending of our publication. Henry Jauhiainen, editor for four years while serving as assistant pastor at Duluth Gospel Tabernacle, now feels that the time demands of his new pastoral work at Cloquet, Minnesota, make it impossible to continue editing and publishing this project."

In 1962, a group of concerned pastors met in a hotel in Estherville, Iowa, to air the need for re-launching a periodical on a cooperative basis. Out of the Estherville meeting, a new form of sponsorship arose.

In January 1963, a new periodical, *Conviction* (now *Fellowship Today*), was launched through the publishing agency of Fellowship Press Corporation. This time, the periodical would be published by an interchurch corporation. Prime responsibility would rest with those churches that chose to become members of the Fellowship Press Corporation.

Thirty-five FCA churches made up this corporation. Paul Zettersten, then pastor of Immanuel Christian Assembly, Los Angeles, California, was selected as editor. He did an outstanding job, faithfully producing this monthly ministry. He and his wife, May, served faithfully for the next 25 years. Rolf Zettersten served as managing editor for many years. In his final editorial (May 1988) as editor, Paul Zettersten wrote: "After several years without a Fellowship periodical, we were searching for a means of common ownership without compromising local church autonomy. Over the past quarter of a century, we have seen this develop."

James and Mary Ellen Mattson became managing editors of *Conviction* magazine (now *Fellowship Today*) beginning with the April 1986 issue. They served faithfully until December 1993.

Time has proven the wisdom of broadening the base of the FCA periodical. Approximately 30 churches in the FCA continue to make up the Fellowship Press Corporation. They elect an 11-person board that provides insight, direction and governance. The board annually elects the editor, managing editor, a president, vice-president, secretary and treasurer. The financial subsidy needed each month to operate in the black is carried equally by the local churches that have chosen to join the corporation. A modest salary is given to the part-time managing editor.

The History of the FCA

In 1988, when Paul Zettersten stepped down as editor, several changes took place. James Mattson became editor, and his wife, Mary Ellen, became assistant editor. An executive committee was established, made up of Lloyd Jacobsen, chairman, along with me, James Mattson and John Sprecher.

In July 1989, the magazine came out with a new format and a new name, *Fellowship Today.* Lloyd Jacobsen, president of Fellowship Press Corporation, wrote the following in his editorial:

> While we hope that your personal convictions will survive and remain strong, you will no longer be receiving *Conviction* magazine. As you will have noticed by now, we have changed the name of our publication to *Fellowship Today.* It is still the same magazine, published by the same group of FCA churches and our commitment to a quality presentation of the activities and message of these churches remains the same, too. We changed the name because we believe *Fellowship Today* reflects more clearly what we are in the Fellowship of Christian Assemblies.
>
> Kittel, the great scholar, defines fellowship as "partnership in work." That definition describes the working of our group of churches very accurately. Although we are a group of independent churches, we also believe in

Sixteen

working together with other churches in a "partnership." We want to avoid, on one hand, the extreme of being totally on our own as local churches, an attitude summed up in the anarchy of Israel during the time of the Judges when "every man did that which was right in his own eyes."

On the other hand, we want to avoid the extreme in church government portrayed shortly after the time of the Judges, when Israel said, "Give us a king so that we may be as other nations." This is a mindset that sees churches advance only when part of a massive, highly organized institution. A well-known church historian once shared with me that his denomination's polity was largely "American Corporate."

At the April 1991 annual FCA convention in Madison, Wisconsin, Jacobsen stepped down, and I was elected as president, Dennis Sawyer vice-president, Richard Doebler secretary and John Sprecher treasurer.

The Mattsons resigned in December 1993, at which time Kim Cortez was appointed managing editor, and I became editor. I continued as editor for many years. It was decided to shorten the 16-page magazine to six pages and call it *FCA Leadership,* and when it was discontinued in favor of an electronic version (an e-zine, also posted on the FCA Web page), Dean Merill began editing it.

The History of the FCA

The six decades of printing ministry reflect the philosophy and theology of the FCA. Interdependence is necessary to the success of independence. A commitment to cooperation must be equally as strong as the commitment to autonomy.

Although independent, almost three decades ago we banded together as a group of churches and established a way to publish this magazine in partnership without infringing on any local church's rights and responsibilities. This was similar to the way we banded together more than 60 years ago and in *partnership* sent out missionaries with the gospel. Since then, we have, as independent churches, planted new churches, owned and operated Bible camps, hosted national conventions, sponsored retreats, supported colleges, facilitated pastoral placement and interchurch ministries and have exercised accountability to one another in ethics and public ministry, all in *partnership* while scrupulously avoiding infringement on any local church's autonomy.

This way of doing things has attracted many new Christian workers and churches to become part of the FCA as evidenced by the remarkable growth we have enjoyed these past years.

The "today" part of *Fellowship Today* suggests that we must stay current and continue

Sixteen

to develop within the framework just described. During the past few years, we have seen in the FCA a growing interest in meeting regularly to discuss and implement the challenge to work even more effectively with each other as independent local churches. The call to evangelize the world and grow the church constrains us to work at finding new ways to enhance our partnership and make it more fruitful in this basic command of God.[33]

Seventeen
Name Change

Following years of debate and discussion, the name was changed from Independent Assemblies of God to the Fellowship of Christian Assemblies in the business session of the annual convention held at the Madison Gospel Tabernacle (now Lake City Church) in Madison, Wisconsin, on May 2, 1973. Our collective identity would be established separate from and non-reactive to the Assemblies of God.

Once again, FCA resolved to remain an informal cooperative fellowship of autonomous local churches, and therefore, the name was not to be incorporated and registered with the government. Each local church would continue to be incorporated and registered with the government for tax purposes. As in past years, we would remain a group without national or international identity, for the most part, or listing in the various handbooks of denominations.

Eighteen
World Outreach Committee – 1980

At the Seattle FCA Convention, May 3, 1980, Roger Anderson was asked to chair a committee to review missions work throughout the FCA and bring recommendations to the 1981 convention.

At the convention on April 30, 1981, in Chicago at the Philadelphia Church, an *ad hoc* committee was chosen from the floor of the convention gathering to make up the World Outreach Committee (WOC) — Roger Anderson, chairman; Ron Brooks, secretary; and, a year later, Barry Crane, treasurer.

The stated purposes were:

1. To facilitate communication among FCA churches concerning missions development and expansion.
2. To provide informative/advisory services to churches and missionaries.
3. To coordinate FCA endeavors in a particular field.
4. To provide regular up-to-date information on World Missions trends and fields of greatest potential.
5. To serve FCA with periodic opportunities for

training of missionaries and local church missions strategy.

After 10 years, the WOC continued to serve missionaries and local churches of the FCA with the resources needed for an ever-expanding vision and outreach into the fields of the world, both at home and abroad. Following the concern for local church distinctiveness, each country of FCA missions endeavor was/is represented by a Fellowship contact church. The contact church is responsible to update the FCA regarding mission changes, missionary status, financial requirements and cultural, political and social changes within the country. In this way, each local contact church serves the Fellowship as a whole. In time, the WOC had separate areas of responsibility — General, Administrative, Urban, Global and Home Missions.

At the annual FCA convention in April 1991, held at Madison Gospel Tabernacle (now Lake City Church), Madison, Wisconsin, the WOC offered a proposal to form a nonprofit corporation, "Fellowship Missions," modeled after the Fellowship Press Corporation, which is responsible for the printing and publishing of *Fellowship Today* magazine. Participation and membership of local churches in Fellowship Missions would be voluntary. The need for a full-time international director to expedite this ministry, travel at home and abroad and help local churches, pastors and missionaries on the field was presented in the business session of the convention. It was

Eighteen

voted to proceed with Fellowship Mission incorporation. Once again, local church autonomy and sovereignty were assured, while teamwork would be implemented. It was terminated the next year because of criticism by ministers who thought it would override the autonomy of the local church's sovereignty.

Nineteen
Fall Fellowship
Concerns Conference

In the summer of 1981, Henry Jauhiainen initiated responses from various FCA pastors regarding their interest in a conference to thoughtfully plan for the future of the Fellowship. The FCA was growing, experiencing greater diversity and receiving inquiries and questions. Theological interest centered around defining who we are and what we believe, exploring ways to preserve unity within diversity, Biblical accountability and new ways of cooperative church planting. The desire was for intentional planning, not knee-jerk reaction to trends, needs and crises.

The first gathering was held in October 1981 in Rockford, Illinois, with about 20 pastors in attendance. A follow-up meeting was held in April 1982, resulting in these clear affirmations:

1. We are totally committed to both local church autonomy and interchurch cooperation as Biblical norms for our life and ministry. In other words, interchurch life and ministry is a Biblical call, not simply an option.
2. We need to define our whole nature and mission as a Fellowship. A clearer

Nineteen

understanding of our whole reason for being will stimulate active interchurch life.

3. We need to see the creation of an ongoing large national task force for Fellowship concerns. This group would meet annually to consider trends, needs and challenges. It would act as a catalyst to stimulate discussions in our annual conventions.

Pastors younger and older expressed great interest in achieving a statement of nature and mission and of commonly held beliefs. For the next five years, heated debates took place on the actual wording of a doctrinal statement of beliefs. It was argued, rewritten, discussed and revised. John Sprecher faithfully chaired these years of meetings, with the help of Lloyd Jacobsen and Wes McLeod. The final draft was presented to the Annual FCA Convention in Banff, Alberta, Canada, in April 1986 and adopted. They have been printed each month in *Conviction* magazine (now *Fellowship Today*), beginning with the June 1986 issue.[34]

Twenty
Directory of Ministers

Over the years, the ministerial listing process was updated, strengthened and clarified repeatedly. Excerpts from various national convention business sessions read as follows:

> Persons desiring to be listed should secure recommendations of two fellowshipping pastors, preferably in their general area, and space for this should be provided on the application form. A local home church should be listed for each person desiring to be listed. The listing of various associations in lieu of a home church is held to be in variance with our convictions.

Emphasis on the local church is an ongoing theme. A common question for identification and credibility is, "What local church do you belong to, and are you in good standing with it?" Secondly, "Are you in good standing with your pastor and the elders of your local church? Can they and will they give you a good recommendation morally, ethically, doctrinally, financially and in regards to your family?"

These questions are not asked of the FCA at large, but of the person's local church and pastor. (See Appendices

Twenty

for application form for the FCA minister's listing of new members.)

The annual Ministerial Directory was (and still is) both a credible and an incredible listing of those in the ministry. It was and still is a challenge to autonomous independent local churches to agree on qualifications for the ministry and disqualifications that remove you from the ministry and, therefore, delete you from being listed in the annual updated publication. An opening paragraph in the current FCA Directory helps explain the situation:

> Please remember that the qualifications for ministry vary from church to church. The home church is responsible for the personal character and discipline of its members.

And the local church also establishes the prerequisites of education and experience required before licensing and ordination. This may vary extensively from one local church to another.

At the annual FCA convention, someone is elected to be the Directory secretary in charge of publishing the next year's updated listing. The current Directory responsibility has been given to Pastor Warren Heckman, Madison, Wisconsin, and his secretary, Nancy Van Maren. They further stated:

> The information contained in this Directory is provided as a ministry to the Fellowship of

The History of the FCA

Christian Assemblies and is based upon responses received from individuals and churches within the FCA. No independent verification has been made of the accuracy or completeness of the responses received, therefore, neither of us in Madison, nor the FCA, assumes responsibility for errors or omissions in compilation and publication of this Directory.

The Biblical principle of Acts 9:26-30 is important in authenticating new ministers into the FCA. Barnabus recommended newly converted Saul of Tarsus to the church at Jerusalem. There is a deep continuous desire that surfaces repeatedly: First, to always adhere to Biblical principles of morality, integrity and doctrinal purity for those serving in ministry; and, second, to allow for the sovereignty of each local church in determining and interpreting those truths, with regards to who can be listed or needs to be deleted from the annual FCA Directory. Thus we have an incredible challenge to maintain a credible listing each year.

Twenty-one
Listing FCA Churches

Over the years, the question of whether we are a Fellowship of ministers or of churches has been debated repeatedly. Obviously we are, in fact, both. Therefore, in the past decade, provision has been made for churches to be listed if they request it. Churches who want to be listed must fill out a form showing that the request comes from their official board. This listing of local churches, like the listing of ministers, is renewed annually. Forms are available through the Fellowship Directory secretary. (See Appendices for sample form.)

The applications for listing by missionaries who are out of the country are either faxed to them for their signatures or signed for them by the respective churches that sent them out.

Some have argued against listing churches because in their minds it is the first step toward denominationalism, organization and loss of autonomy and sovereignty of the local church. Who will have the authority to decide who can be listed and who cannot?

The opposite opinion is that if we are already cooperating together, let us at least know one another and be able to work better as a team. The listing provides invaluable information for cooperative ministry and missionary itinerary. After all, the autonomy of the local church is exercised in the decision whether to be listed or not.

Growth was rapid between 1982 and 1986. The number of individuals listed grew from 286 to 429, a 50 percent increase. The listing of churches grew from 137 to 173, a 26 percent increase.

By 1994, there were 573 individuals listed in the FCA Directory and 203 local churches. Yet, a careful perusal of the listings from year to year shows quite a number who were not listed for a year or two and then were listed again. Probably some forgot to fill out the annual form, and when the deadline passed, they were excluded. Others chose not to be listed, wanting to make a statement, unhappy with one aspect or another of the FCA. And, finally, although the FCA has consistently grown over the years, pastors and churches continue to move on and join other groups.

The ambiguity of autonomy and the animosity often expressed at the thought of losing autonomy clash continually in annual business sessions. Though good-spirited debate is generally the result, it has been a constant hindrance to accomplishing the greater tasks that necessitate teamwork. (This is the author's personal opinion.) Whether it is a copout for not committing to a joint project, a camouflage for stubborn independence and noninvolvement or a conviction based on Biblical understanding, united efforts have regularly lost out in the long run. It is my own understanding that the latter is a misunderstanding of what scripture says about

Twenty-one

independence and interdependence, accountability and responsibility, synergism not the "sinner-ism" of sharing in serving.

Those who become interested in the FCA ask, "What do I have to do to join? What are the requirements, and how do I join?" For a number of years, we had no commonly held statement of beliefs, statement of purpose or written history. The ambiguity of autonomy and animosity of losing it negated many from further inquiry. When asked, "What do you believe as a group?" we had to stutter and mutter, "Well, you know, what most other evangelical/Pentecostal groups believe."

So the question remained, "How do I join?" The answer: "Hang around, attend area Fellowship meetings, the Annual National Convention, subscribe to *Fellowship Today* magazine, fill out a form to be listed in the FCA Directory and have two of your FCA pastor friends sign it."

This was not all bad, but it certainly is not all good, either. After years of committee work, debate, modification and change, we arrived at an acceptable statement of who we are and what we believe. This was especially meaningful to younger ministers and those new to the FCA. It has also been very beneficial in local churches when explaining to visitors who we are, where we are coming from and what we believe. (See Appendices for FCA Statement of Beliefs.)

Twenty-two
Clarification of Credentialing Certificates

A uniformity in the forms used for credentialing ministers and missionaries was presented and accepted by the FCA convention in Chicago, Illinois, June 10-11, 1970. Various churches had used a number of different forms, sizes and wordings until this time.

This would not change the fact that each local church was responsible for setting standards of training, experience, doctrine, moral and ethical qualifications for licensing and ordaining. They also would be responsible for the ongoing nurture and, if necessary, discipline of those they ordained.

Twenty-three
Booklet on the Fellowship

At the 1958 FCA convention (Ministers' Institute) in St. Paul, Minnesota, a formal request was made for a written pamphlet describing the way of life followed by the FCA (then Independent Assemblies of God). Many requests had been made by numerous people through the years, both for distribution within their local churches and to give to the many inquiries from pastors and churches that were looking for interchurch action and accountability without loss of local church independence and sovereignty.

The history and working process of the Fellowship was defined in a booklet written in 1959 by E.C. Erickson and Henry Jauhiainen, entitled *Independent Assemblies of God — An Experience in Inter-Church Fellowship*. It was updated several times and was finally succeeded by *The Fellowship of Christian Assemblies United States Handbook*, written by Henry Jauhiainen and Richard Doebler, 1992, Philadelphia Press, Seattle, Washington.

Twenty-four
Camps

Christian camp ministry has a long history within the FCA. Camps are held during the summer for children, middle school, high school and families in various areas of the country. Through the years, campgrounds have been rented and, in some cases, purchased. FCA churches have joined together forming nonprofit corporations to accomplish the ownership of campgrounds and further develop them. Retreats are held throughout the year for singles, couples, men, women and youth.

Twenty-five
Mission Outreach

From the beginning, new churches have been planted in a variety of ways. Entrepreneurial evangelists have established churches singlehandedly. Sensing God's leading to a certain city, they started preaching, plus working at secular employment until enough people gathered together to support them. Other churches have been born through an established mother church's outreach, support and vision. Cooperative ventures have brought together several churches, which share in the investment of time, personnel and money until a new work is self-supporting and self-governing as an autonomous local church.

Foreign mission outreach is closely tied to the local church. There are numerous churches that have annual missions conventions and missions policies. Larger churches are able to send and solely support their own missionaries, while most churches need the cooperative help of other local churches to accomplish this task. Missionaries, like others going into the ministry, are educated, evaluated, equipped and trained according to the standards established by their home church. Their home church ordains them and commissions them for full-time ministry and establishes the guidelines, parameters and time frame of their mission. Missionaries must usually itinerate among churches to raise adequate support.

The oversight, administration and evaluation of missionaries are all handled through their home church and not through a state or national headquarters. Thus, an advantage is that there is a higher ratio of going to giving. In most cases, 100 percent of what is given goes to missions. Local churches act in the capacity of denominational officials in an administrative office. Money needed to build, maintain and equip a national headquarters is eliminated, as are salaries for such people. The disadvantages are basically in the added workload, cost and necessity of local churches and pastors to be actively involved with their missionaries, visiting them on the field for updates, evaluation and decision making.

Twenty-six
History of the Founding
of Leading FCA Churches

The Pentecostal movement or outpouring of the Holy Spirit came to hungry hearts in many places of the world on or before the turn of the century. Older believers in Fosston, Minnesota, testify of parents being baptized in the Holy Spirit, speaking in tongues and the miraculous taking place before 1900. Records are almost nonexistent, but stories have been passed on by word of mouth.

In order to get a broader picture of the beginning of the Independent Assemblies of God (now FCA), I contacted numerous churches, asking for their histories. I have included the histories of those Fellowship churches that responded.

Some were already functioning local churches that heard this new message, accepted it and became Pentecostal churches. Some were born out of prayer meetings that gave birth to a local church upon receiving the baptism in the Holy Spirit. Early pastoral leaders in the FCA are mentioned repeatedly in histories of our first churches. Many of them served in several of the young Pentecostal churches.

The History of the FCA

Philadelphia Church
Seattle, Washington – 1901

In April 1901, Tobias Tonnesen, accompanied by his family, left the Midwestern state of Wisconsin, where they had been living and Tonnesen had been lay-ministering, and moved to the Pacific Northwest. The Tonnesen family settled on land located in the small city of Ballard, Washington, in the area around Salmon Bay. They rented an upstairs apartment between 20th N.W. and 22nd N.W., which was then called "Crawford" Street and is now known as N.W. 59th Street.

Tobias Tonnesen soon became acquainted with a number of other brethren who, like himself, did not feel at home in the established denominational churches. They longed for the founding of a free and independent work. This group began to have cottage prayer meetings in the Tonnesens' upstairs apartment. Not many months later, a lot was purchased and a house built by the Tonnesens on Chestnut Street (now known as N.W. 61st) near 17th N.W. Meetings were held there, in addition to other homes. As the Lord blessed, the small group that met together grew to about 12 families. They were an open-minded assemblage of brethren and desired to possess all that God had for them. The group identified themselves with no specific denomination, but referred to themselves simply as "Free People."

In the year 1902, R.G. Rasmussen (a convert of a northern Minnesota revival meeting) left Superior,

Wisconsin, for Ballard and began to assist T.E. Tonnesen in leading the home Bible studies and services.

R.G. Rasmussen and T.E. Tonnesen were the two human instruments the Lord used in the establishment of the early pioneer work in Ballard, which eventually became the Philadelphia Church.

With the increasing attendance of the cottage prayer meetings in the latter part of 1904, homes had become inadequate to accommodate the gatherings. For a short time, the group rented a vacant schoolhouse on lower Sunset Hill to meet the need for more room. In 1905, a lot was purchased in the 6500 block on Jones Avenue, and the men of the church banded together to construct a little church, which became known as the Jones Avenue Mission. Even though "regular" denominational structure did not appeal to the people of the Mission, they desired some sort of organization within the body. Therefore, a business meeting was held, three trustees were elected and a constitution adopted consisting of a portion of the Word of God, which seemed most suitable to the congregation. The selection of this particular scriptural passage seems to have proven prophetical in nature since the Jones Avenue Mission became possibly the first Pentecostal assembly as such in the Seattle area. That portion was I Corinthians 12, 13 and 14 — word for word.

In the fall of 1906, the Jones Avenue Mission received a letter from an evangelist named Strand who had previously held meetings at the young assembly. The content of that letter was the catalyst which completely changed the Mission. Brother Strand's letter came from the Los Angeles area where he had been visiting for some time. He had been attending the Azusa Street Mission and had a glowing story to report. Brother Tonnesen read the letter to the congregation. It told of how the Mission was a place where a group of hungry souls began to pour out their hearts to God and to seek His face. Brother Strand explained in his letter how the Lord had met the seeking folks with a blessed Holy Spirit outpouring, many were saved and people had been healed from various sicknesses. In the process of Brother Strand's visits to the Azusa Street Mission, he became exceedingly hungry to be filled with the Holy Spirit as recorded in Acts 2:4. Then he told how, after he sought the face of God, he had experienced the baptism in the Holy Spirit. Oh, the joy that had become his portion … oh, the deep assurance of the reality of God which filled his heart. The Holy Spirit had also given him such power to witness. He wrote that he wished there were some way that he could tell in words of the glory that was his, but all he could do was praise God for giving him that which Jesus Christ referred to as "the promise of the Father."

When Brother Tonnesen finished reading the letter, the congregation sat in awe and wonder and began to hunger for the fullness of the Holy Spirit. They all agreed that what Brother Strand had written about was what the Jones Avenue Mission needed. The people of the Mission began to seek God, and the Holy Ghost revival broke out. This was in the month of October 1906. Other believers in

Twenty-six

the city came running to the Mission after hearing the revival reports. The people realized their tiny Mission was not adequate for the crowds that were coming, so on Thanksgiving Day 1906, the west wall of the church building was torn down, and the building was enlarged to nearly twice its size. Three days later, it is said, the enlarged building was used for services!

The years 1908-1920 were years of progress for the Jones Avenue Mission. The Lord continued to bless as the people continued to pray to and praise God.

In the spring of 1920, the assembly was dealt a disheartening blow — the Jones Avenue Mission burned to the ground! The church building, all of the furnishings, all their hard work (plus the funds that went into it) went up in flames. The actual cause of the blaze remains a mystery, although arson has been suspected.

Without a church building, they rented an old Baptist church on West 56th Street. Because the congregation was no longer located on Jones Avenue, the Mission was renamed the Scandinavian Pentecostal Mission.

In late 1920, Einar J. Holm, an evangelist from Canada, came to minister for a time. He remained on as "acting pastor" during 1921.

In 1922, the assembly, hitherto classified as a "volunteer organization," decided it was time to officially incorporate themselves under the laws of the State of Washington. Therefore, the current membership roll of the Volunteer Scandinavian Pentecostal Mission of Ballard was adopted as the membership roll of the

The History of the FCA

Scandinavian Pentecostal Mission, Inc.

The spring of 1922 brought a new leader. Elder K.G. Stolsen was requested by the church board to remain with the church and be their "Elder in Charge," with Brother Rasmussen as Associate Elder. Brother Stolsen agreed to the proposition. The board agreed that since Brother Stolsen would not be working otherwise, the church should support him. Thus, Karl G. Stolsen became the first paid pastor of the church.

When Pastor Stolsen gave notice of his desire to resign in early 1925, a Swedish brother by the name of Ernest Nilsson arrived with his family in the States in October and assumed the pastorate the same month. The Stolsens moved to Tacoma and assumed a pastorate there. Pastor Nilsson resigned in September 1929. Rev. Arthur F. Johnson, a pastor, missionary, evangelist, Bible teacher and singer, agreed to come and "interim" at the church for six months in their time of real need. Brother Johnson, his wife, Beatrice, and son, Philip, arrived in April of 1930.

After about three months of filling in as pastor, Brother A.F. Johnson was voted in by an almost unanimous vote as permanent pastor.

There was fundamental progress in various areas of the church under Pastor A.F. Johnson's ministry. The name of the church was again changed, this time to the Scandinavian Pentecostal Tabernacle from Scandinavian Pentecostal Mission. Formal church bylaws were suggested, discussed and written during that first year of Pastor Johnson's leadership.

Twenty-six

In January 1933, led to return to the Midwest and go into evangelistic work and sensing that the church was in good condition, the Johnsons submitted their resignation, effective in June. Their resignation was accepted with reluctance.

Arvid Ohrnell, from Chicago, accepted the pastorate and arrived to assume this new charge on June 27, 1933. Pastor Ohrnell surprised the church when, at the assembly meeting of December 1935, he tendered his resignation, effective in March 1936.

During the interim, before a new permanent pastor was chosen, Carl Anderson served as temporary pastor, and then B.M. Johnson was acting pastor for seven months.

In February 1937, a five-night joint evangelistic crusade was held in the old Metropolitan Theater with the renowned Pentecostal pioneer Levi Petrus of Stockholm, Sweden, as the guest speaker. Two churches cooperated with the Scandinavian Pentecostal Tabernacle in this venture — Hollywood Temple and Fremont Pentecostal Tabernacle (now known as Calvary Temple and Westminster Assembly, respectively). This series of meetings was a real uplift to the members of the church, a spiritual and a financial success.

The welcoming service for the next permanent pastor of the assembly was held June 14, 1937. Rev. M.J. Hagli and his family were from Tacoma, Washington, and had been missionaries to China.

One of the first orders of business was again to change

the name of the church. On January 1, 1938, the assembly was officially incorporated as the Ballard Pentecostal Tabernacle. Special services during 1937 included meetings with converted opera tenor Elinar Waermo and with the Fox Evangelistic party.

In the January 1939 annual assembly meeting, Pastor Hagli announced that he was resigning.

During the seven months that followed, the church struggled along with guest speakers and various members of the church taking turns in the pulpit. In the August 1939 assembly meeting, Rev. C. Albert Moseid of Superior, Wisconsin, was chosen as pastor by an almost unanimous vote.

In February of 1947, Pastor Moseid announced his resignation, which was to be effective June 15, 1947. Noteworthy progress was experienced by the church during Pastor Moseid's more than seven-year tenure as shepherd of the Tabernacle flock. During this time, the church's membership had more than doubled, and the financial situation was sound.

The members were eager for a new pastor to be decided upon and called someone very quickly so that the new pastor could be welcomed as soon as possible following Brother Moseid's departure.

The call to pastor the Ballard Pentecostal Tabernacle was extended to Rev. Roy C. Johnson. Brother Johnson, who had pastored in Michigan, "interimed" at Immanuel Christian Assembly in Los Angeles and was serving as an evangelist. He was a good friend of Rev. E.C. Erickson of the Duluth Gospel Tabernacle, with whom he had also worked. Pastor Erickson had also been called to serve as pastor of the Ballard church in the 1930s, but had declined. Brother Johnson accepted the call and was welcomed, along with his wife, Viola, and daughter, Donna, on Sunday, June 25, 1947. According to Pastor Johnson, who recalled this 30 years later, there were about 50 people present that first Sunday evening.

Almost immediately upon Rev. Johnson's assumption of the pastorate, the church began to branch out into new fields of service.

First, a one-year contract with a Seattle radio station, KOL, was secured for a half-hour program originating every Sunday afternoon from the church auditorium as soon as the required electronic equipment could be obtained and installed.

Second, Harold and Grace Hestekind were sent as the church's representatives to the land of China — the church's first fully supported foreign missionaries, leaving March 21, 1948.

Third, a fund was established and a committee created to undertake the planning and building of a new church sanctuary.

Fourth, another name change was necessary. While the assembly was called the Ballard Pentecostal Tabernacle, another church in the area was known as the Ballard Gospel Tabernacle, which caused confusion to the nearby residents and post office. Two names were presented to the church for their vote. The first name suggested was the

"Philadelphia Church," after the church of Philadelphia referred to in the book of Revelation. The other name optioned was "Beulah Temple." A standing vote was taken on the name "Philadelphia Church," and it was unanimously accepted. The church was officially incorporated under this name on January 8, 1948.

The official dedication of the new church building was held on Sunday, January 13, 1952. Rev. Harry Stemme of Los Angeles was the guest speaker, and Hilding Halvarson and Sven Bjork were the guest soloists. Rev. Roy Johnson served as pastor for 30 years, retiring in 1977.

In 1977, Paul Zettersten answered the call to be pastor of Philadelphia Church. The present Pastor is Derek Forseth.[36]

Bethel Christian Assembly
Tacoma, Washington – 1906

Bethel Christian Assembly has a unique and rich heritage, with its roots in the Pentecostal Revival of the early 1900s. House meetings began in 1906, and in the summer of 1907, tent meetings were held at 11th and Cushman in Tacoma. The meetings then continued next door at the Free Mission Hall. The congregation of this early church was comprised mainly of Norwegian immigrants.

In1926, more immigrants arrived from Norway and Sweden. It was now time for the group to consider formal church membership, and a meeting was called in

Twenty-six

September 1926 for that purpose. Anton Nilsen was chairman of that meeting. The group took the name The Scandinavian Mission and called their first pastor, Rev. Stolson. In addition, the first three deacons were chosen: John Kvamme, Ole Snartemo and K.J. Konsmo. Two of these family names are still represented in their church body.

During the succeeding three years, The Scandinavian Mission continued to flourish, ministering to the community in their native Norwegian language. Following Rev. Stolson's departure, Rev. Lunquist was called to serve. In March 1929, the congregation moved to the church building at the corner of 11th and "J" and remained there until 1973. Rev. Lunquist (1927-1929) and Rev. Jens Gustavsen (1929-1932) led The Scandinavian Mission until the arrival of Rev. A.W. Rasmussen in 1933. During his ministry, the church changed its name from The Scandinavian Mission to Bethel Pentecostal Assembly and began to minister to the English-speaking people in Tacoma, in addition to its Scandinavian membership. The church enjoyed steady growth during this period of time.

Pastor Rasmussen resigned in 1936 and was succeeded by Rev. Carl Hedeen (1936-1940) and then Rev. John Mosied. During Pastor Mosied's eight-year ministry, there was a special move of the Holy Spirit, particularly among the young people. Rev. Mosied suffered a stroke in 1948, after which the church was led by a number of interim pastors (including Rev. Winston Nunes) until 1953, when Pastor Rasmussen was called back to serve. In 1962, an associate, G.H. Nunn, was called to assist with pastoral responsibilities. Pastor Nunn assumed full pastoral duties in 1963 upon the resignation of Rev. Rasmussen.

Meanwhile in 1953, Tacoma Gospel Assembly was organized under the leadership of Clifford Johnson. Following Rev. Johnson's departure, Ernest Maisch (1955-1967) served and was succeeded by Rev. Wesley Braaten, who assumed pastoral duties in 1967. (Rev. Braaten is the father of one of their deacon's wife, Jane Zetterberg.) Pastor Braaten and Pastor Nunn thought it would be good for the two churches to join as one fellowship; each approached his respective board and congregation, and in 1968, the two congregations joined together. A resolution was made that a new building be erected.

The church congregation spent three years constructing the building themselves, going into little debt. Construction was completed in April 1973, and the congregation moved in immediately. Dedication of the building took place in September 1973, with praise and thanksgiving to God for what He had done! This new building (their current facility) was erected on the site of the old Tacoma Gospel Assembly, and the old Bethel church was sold to another Pentecostal congregation. The church adopted a new name, Bethel Christian Assembly, and began its new ministry.

Known as the "Christ is the Answer" church, Bethel has flourished under the following leadership: Pastors Wesley Braaten (1967-1974), Del Jester (1975-1981) and Nils Leksen (1981-1988). Their current pastor, William

Wolfson, became the senior pastor in March 1989. The Lord has blessed Bethel Christian Assembly with tremendous growth, both physically and spiritually.[37]

Lake View Gospel Church
Chicago, Illinois – 1910

Many people have fond memories of the humble beginning of Lake View Gospel Church. It was affectionately called the "Old Barry Avenue Church" in the early days of Pentecost in Chicago.

Before 1908, many old-timers, including Oscar and John Frizen, Nels Anderson and others, received the infilling of the Holy Spirit, according to Acts 2:4. They came from various denominations and gathered together for prayer and worship in private homes. Soon there was a need for a permanent place of worship.

The Methodist church building on Kenmore and Barry Avenues was bought and moved to 944 Barry Avenue in 1898 by Nels Anderson, as the Methodists were building a new church. The Andersons used this building for a tailoring business and later offered "rent-free" space to the now growing congregation who were still without a permanent church home.

A short time later, Rev. B.M. Johnson, a graduate of a Baptist Seminary in Duluth, Minnesota, became the first pastor and served faithfully for 25 years. Previously, Brother Johnson had come to Chicago and received the baptism of the Holy Spirit, causing his dismissal from the

The History of the FCA

Baptist church in northern Michigan where he had pastored.

The church first met on Sunday afternoons, but soon changed to a full schedule of services — all in the Swedish language. The name officially chosen was Svenska Pingst Forsamlingen (Swedish Pentecostal Assembly). The church name was changed several times — The Swedish Assembly of God and later to Lake View Gospel Church.

This young church was to become known all over the world and often was crowded to the doors with people standing during the services. From this church there were those who braved many experiences of those early days on the mission field.

Going out from "Old Barry Avenue" as early missionaries were Brothers Vingren and Berg to Brazil, South America; the Otto Nelsons to Brazil and Uruguay; Carrie Anderson to China and after 12 years in China to Singapore and later to Malaya; and revival meetings and many thousands of souls saved and numerous churches opened in Brazil through the Nels Nelson family supported by Lake View since their first contact in 1919. The Lake View Gospel Church also had a part in prayer and financial support with numerous other individuals and missions projects, including the Missionary Rest Home on the northwest side of Chicago, Assemblies of God Children's Home in Maryville, Illinois, Evangelical Child and Family Association, etc. Of course, the Home of Onesiphorous (now known as "Kids Alive") was always of great interest to Lake View friends after Florence and Al

Lunmark began their full-time ministry for the Home in 1928.

The Lord blessed, and the congregation continued to meet at the Barry Avenue quarters (still rent free) until the new church building at 1331 North Racine Avenue was built and ready to be occupied. A parade of saints walked together from the Barry Avenue church all the way to the brand new church building for the first service in 1928. Prior to this time, the services were in Swedish, and they sang from a special songbook, compiled by Pastor B.M. Johnson called *Lovsangs Toner*. At this time, the church services added English to their Swedish services in the new Racine Avenue church.

According to the Lake View bylaws adopted by the members, deacons were elected and served for a given period of time. Special provision was made for men of God — through their spiritual life and faithful service to the church and the Lord in all walks of life — to be noted as elders. Lake View Gospel Church had two such men who were honored in this capacity, Brother Oscar S. Frizen and Rev. G.A. Lundmark, who served many years. As elders of the church, they also assisted the pastors in many matters.

Those who served as pastors were: Rev. B.M. Johnson (1910-1935), Rev. John A. Westman (1935-1945), Dr. C.C. Burnett (1945-1948), Rev. DeVore H. Walterman (1948-1952), Rev. Arthur M. Johnson (1952-1962), Rev. Leland Paulson (1962-1967) and Rev. Clarence Fast (1967-1970).

As the years passed, Lake View Gospel Church was not

meeting the needs of the influx of the Cuban and Spanish-speaking people who were now living near and around the church. Those who attended the church felt that this mission field could best be met by their own people. It was brought to the church leaders' attention that a Cuban pastor was endeavoring to start a church work in the Lake View area. The Open Bible Fellowship group and the leaders of Lake View met. The proceeds of the sale of "dear old Swedish Lake View Gospel Church" were dispersed to several organizations and individuals, including Missionary Martha Schoonmaker, Chicago Bible College, Faith Tabernacle and others.

The last service of the church was held in December 1970. So, after 62 years of good, faithful ministry, the Lake View Gospel Church came to a close and passed the torch to the Spanish and Cuban brethren who continue preaching in the Lake View area.[38]

Homewood Full Gospel Church
Homewood, Illinois – 1911

Homewood Full Gospel Church was founded in the early 1900s. It was established as West Auburn Park Swedish Baptist Church on January 2, 1911. The church, owned by the congregation, was located at 1109 West 69th Street in Chicago.

In 1922, the name was changed to West Auburn Park Church when it became an independent Full Gospel church. On April 1, 1930, the West Auburn Park Church moved to a large store at 5850 South Halsted Street, changing the name to Swedish Assembly of God, independent of the Assemblies of God denomination. They moved because of the heavy Swedish population at the Halsted Street area.

The Swedish Assembly of God moved from the Halsted Street location in about 1930 to a large building (formerly known as Chatham Theatre) at 7546 Cottage Grove Avenue. Another congregation known as the Grand Crossing Swedish Pentecostal Church joined with the Swedish Assembly of God at the new location.

In about 1931, the congregation moved to a store at 445 East 75th Street. While at this location, services were often held at the gymnasium of the Wakeford Methodist Church, St. Lawrence Avenue at East 76th Street.

In 1940, the congregation purchased property and built a new church building at 740 East 77th Street. On October 11, 1940, the name was changed to Beulah Temple.

In 1955, the church was sold to a Baptist congregation. From 1955 to 1957, the church rented the K.P. Hall at 11037 South Michigan Avenue. In 1957, the congregation purchased property at 11325 South Halsted Street and built a church. On October 12, 1958, the name was changed to Beulah Gospel Temple.

This building was sold to a Church of Christ in 1971, as most of the congregation had moved to the south suburbs. From 1971 to 1973, the congregation met in three locations: the Dixie Governor Motel on Dixie

The History of the FCA

Highway in East Hazel Crest; the Church of the Master at Kedzie Avenue and Fossmoor Road; and Homewood Flossmoor High School. During this transition, the name was changed to Homewood Full Gospel Church.

The present property at 18620 South Kedzie Avenue in Homewood was purchased, and a new building was built and occupied on October 7, 1973. They were blessed by tremendous growth from the Lord. Thus, in 1985, the new auditorium (seating for more than 2,000 people) was built around the existing church building and occupied in March 1987.

Over these years, many ministers and missionaries were thrust out into the field, both nationally and internationally through the church. Homewood Full Gospel Church has been blessed by the ministry of great pastors: Petrus Swartz (1911-1925), Arthur F. Johnson (1925-1930), David Lundquist (1930-1932), Arthur F. Johnson (1932-1933), M.F. Johnson (1933-1935), S. Paul Carlyss (1935-1947), Clair D. Hutchins (1947-1953), Jack Whitesell (1953-1965), Earl Bergman (1965-1969), Walter Pedersen (1969-1991) and George K. Thomas (1991-2007).

The name was changed to All Nations Community Church in the mid-1980s.[39]

Duluth Gospel Tabernacle
Duluth, Minnesota – 1916

The "Macedonian call" that brought the first full

Twenty-six

gospel messengers to Duluth in 1908 came not from a man, as in Paul's vision, but from a woman. A Presbyterian minister's wife, whose heart hungered for the deeper things of God, appealed to the leaders of the little Full Gospel Mission on Ogden Avenue across the bay. In response to that appeal, Pentecost came, not only to that Presbyterian minister's wife and husband, but also to Duluth.

The first messengers, a Brother Bardon and a Brother Lee, opened the first little Full Gospel Mission on Superior Street, a few doors west of the present church site. For the next several years, there was only an intermittent Pentecostal testimony in the city. In 1913, a Rev. Neve and a Rev. Emery opened meetings in the flat-iron building at Superior and Michigan Street, but after two years, moved on to other fields.

The year 1915 was a dark year for the little mission. Left without pastoral help, the little flock scattered. It looked as if the Full Gospel Mission light would be extinguished. But the following year, in answer to the prayers of the few faithful remaining members, God sent an evangelist with a shepherd's heart. Rev. and Mrs. Arthur F. Johnson set to work gathering the scattered remnants and establishing them in the faith. Under their leadership, the little group increased in numbers and became incorporated as a local church in 1916.

During this two-year period, services were held in two different locations: first at 1628 West Superior Street and then at 1710 Piedmont Avenue.

The History of the FCA

In 1918, Brother Johnson resigned his pastorate and, together with his wife, sailed for the eastern European missionary fields.

Again the little group was left without a shepherd, and again in answer to prayer, God sent Pastor and Mrs. E.C. Erickson in the fall of 1918.

By 1920, the assembly had outgrown its little mission hall at 1710 Piedmont Avenue and moved back to Superior Street — this time into a church building. The period of rented mission halls was past. The assembly now had a church home.

Although the Second Presbyterian building, which they had now secured, was only a little frame structure and badly in need of repairs, it seemed commodious to a congregation that had always worshiped inside the four bare walls of little mission halls. The feeling of permanence seemed to pervade the place and began to reflect itself in the people who attended the gatherings. Instead of being looked upon as a "fly-by-night affair," both friend and foe began to accept the Pentecostal folks as permanent fixtures.

By 1927, the congregation had again outgrown its quarters. In November, they broke ground for the first unit of its present building. For several years, this new unit was used in conjunction with the old building. In 1934, the old part was torn down, and a new structure arose in its place. A few years later, a circular balcony was installed, increasing the seating capacity to approximately 1,000.

E.C. Erickson continued as senior pastor until 1964,

when Henry Jauhiainen took over. Jauhiainen served from 1964 to 1974. Since then, the senior pastors serving the church include: Paul Johnson, George Stormont, Leland Paulson and Tom Kennington. Assistant pastors have included Philip Johnson, David Morken, Henry Jauhiainen, G.J. Flokstra, Lloyd Jacobsen, Richard Carlson, Dennis Forehand, Ron Brooks, Sidney Peterson and Emily Larson.[40] The present pastor is Rolf Fure.

Philadelphia Church
Chicago, Illinois – 1925

During the summer of 1924, a family which belonged to the Methodist church in Chicago returned to Sweden for a short visit. While there, they met a minister who had a great burden on his heart to come to Chicago. Recognizing the call of God in the matter, they encouraged him to come.

There were many young Swedish people who had migrated to the United States and settled in Chicago. A great number were from homes of prayer. When Rev. Arvid Ohrnell came to the States in the summer of 1925, he desired to open a mission to reach these young people.

At the same time, a group of believers meeting regularly in homes prayed for a church with the Bible pattern that they knew so well. Many of them had been won for the Lord through the efforts of the Pentecostal people in Sweden. Many had received their own experience of the baptism with the Holy Spirit while living or visiting in Sweden. Several had been filled with the Spirit in the Chicago area. They were not satisfied in assemblies where truth of "local church order" and the "present ministry of the Holy Spirit" were not accepted. With the great hunger for more of God and a burden for a work in Chicago, prayer meetings were held as often as possible in order to seek God in regards to these things.

With the coming of Rev. Ohrnell, a meeting place was rented at 3315 North Clark Street and opened for public meetings in November 1925. The Filadelfia Mission was opened by Eric Peterson (the one who had gone to visit Sweden in 1924) with Rev. Ohrnell in charge of the services. The friends who had been praying for a Biblical assembly now met in this place, believing it to be the leading of the Lord and an answer to their prayers.

For the first few months, Arvid Ohrnell and Victor Norlin led the work. In January, Rev. Efraim Fraim came to Chicago. He was asked to stay and minister to the people until a Biblical assembly could be organized.

The people chose Sunday, March 7, 1926 to organize and set in order the assembly. Many ministers and friends were invited to this occasion. Rev. Fraim led the meeting and the organization of the assembly. Thirty-two members united together in assembly.

The new assembly took the name of Filadelfiaforsamlingen. Rev. Fraim was given a unanimous call to become its pastor. He accepted the call and served as pastor until the spring of 1930, when he returned home to Sweden.

Twenty-six

In the beginning of May, it was necessary for the church to move. Various halls and buildings were rented for the public meetings, and prayer meetings were held in the members' homes.

Among the buildings used were Trumbull School and the community hall of the bank building at 5437 North Clark Street, which prophetically was to become the present home of the church.

On November 14, 1926, the first church building owned by the congregation was dedicated. It was located at 3300 North Sheffield Avenue.

On March 10, 1927, the church voted to incorporate under the laws of the State of Illinois. An English name was necessary, so it was decided to change the name to Philadelphia Swedish Pentecostal Church.

Rev. Carl Hedeen came to the city in the fall of 1929, along with Rev. Alfred Gustafson. Upon the request of Pastor Fraim, Rev. Hedeen was asked to accept the call as pastor of the church and served until the spring of 1933.

Rev. Joseph Mattsson (Boze) of the Smyrna Assembly of Gothenburg, Sweden, was extended a call in the summer of 1933. During the time between Rev. Hedeen and the coming of Rev. Mattsson, the church was served by Evangelists David Karlsson and Sven Linden.

In the fall of 1934, the Salem Church of Evanston merged with the Philadelphia Church. It was a coming together sanctioned by the memberships.

The church continued to grow until it was necessary to hold the special meetings, revivals, conventions, etc. at larger meeting halls. Many halls and school auditoriums were used during these special efforts. Tent meetings were held for many summers on the north side.

Rev. K.G. Stolsen of Seattle ministered in the church several months in 1934 and again in 1935, when Pastor Mattsson went to Sweden to marry. Rev. Stolsen died in 1940.

Rev. Gosta Schmidt was called from Sweden to become assistant pastor and stringband leader. He was welcomed into the ministry of the church in March 1936. He served faithfully until November 1938, at which time he returned to Sweden. At the same time, Rev. Mattsson resigned the church to accept the call at Rock Church, New York City.

Rev. Arvid Bramwall was invited to fill the vacancy until a permanent pastor was called. Rev. Victor Norlin also helped during this time.

Rev. Oliver Pethrus was called to be assistant pastor and stringband leader. He was welcomed in August 1939 and served faithfully until December 1941.

In September 1939, Dr. Harry Lindblom was called as pastor. He accepted but due to illness was unable to serve until the spring of 1940. He never fully regained his health and went to be with the Lord in the early summer.

Due to the growth of the church, the building at 3300 North Sheffield Avenue was far too small. It was necessary for the Sunday services to be held in special rented halls. At that time, the bank building at 5437 North Clark Street was made available, and it was purchased in July 1939. After extensive alterations, it was converted into what is now their present church building. The dedication was held in March 1940.

Rev. Carl Anderson, a visiting minister from Sweden, labored in the church, both during the illness and after the death of Dr. Lindblom.

In September 1940, a call was extended to Rev. Lewi Pethrus. He accepted the pastoral call for three years. Due to war conditions, he was unable to come until March 1941 and then could not bring his wife and whole family along, just his two younger sons. Under these conditions, he labored in the church until the first of July. He asked to be released due to the war conditions in Europe and the burden for his family. In September, he returned to Sweden.

During the first 15 years, the services for the most part were in the Swedish language. However, as more of the American-born young people began to take part, it was considered wise to have both English and Swedish, with the gatherings slowly changing to all English-speaking services.

Rev. A.W. Rasmussen was called as pastor in November 1941. In the beginning of 1942, Rev. August Lindholm was asked to be assistant pastor and stringband leader. He served until May 1943. Rev. Mattsson was called as co-pastor of the church and took up his duties in April of 1943. January of 1944, Rev. Rasmussen resigned to pioneer a work in Edmonton, Alberta, Canada. The church sponsored this as a home mission project for one year.

The History of the FCA

In November 1946, Rev. Harry Ring was asked to take over the church while Pastor Mattsson was in Mexico and Sweden. He was welcomed as associate pastor in February 1947. He continued in this capacity until he resigned to accept the pastorate at Jamestown, New York, August 28, 1948.

Since the church at Edmonton was established and growing, Rev. A.W. Rasmussen was asked to help in the church during Pastor Mattsson's trip to the Scandinavian countries.

In June 1950, he returned to minister in the Philadelphia Church as associate pastor. He served the church in this office until June 19, 1954, at which time he went to Bethel Assembly in Tacoma, Washington. During this time, he started Chicago Bible College as a full-time school. Before this, the training sessions had been short-term periods in conjunction with the annual conventions of the Independent Assemblies of God.

In the fall of 1954, Charles Allen was called to be music and youth director. At the same time, Dr. Russell Meade was called to be in charge of Chicago Bible College and minister in the church. In the spring of 1956, the church decided that the Chicago Bible College was to be separate from the church.

For several years, Pastor Mattsson had a burden for East Africa. In June 1955, he spent several weeks there. He was unable to return before the early spring of 1958, and training classes for the natives were started. He resigned from local church duties in December 1956 in order to

Twenty-six

follow God's leading. He remained pastor until August 10, 1958.

Dr. Meade was asked to be interim pastor until a new pastor could be called. He was voted as pastor on June 16, 1959. Rev. Daryl Merrill was called to work with the stringband and young people the first part of 1961. For Scandinavian people, having a stringband was a very important ingredient to worship.

After Dr. Meade, the church was served over the years by Pastor Bob Anderson, followed by Pastor Dennis Sawyer, Pastor Don Impaglia, Pastor Jack Holm and James Revelle.[41] This church is now pastored by an interim pastor.

Lake City Church
Madison, Wisconsin – 1927

The Madison Gospel Tabernacle was born during the Great Depression days. The work began as a small mission effort on the east side of Madison, Wisconsin, in 1927 under the leadership of Miss Sophie Pfankuchen, a former missionary to Africa. In the early days, the group invited Paul Rader to conduct a service. This well-known Chicago preacher had a good influence on the community, and several were converted. The growth led the group to call their first pastor in 1931, Rev. W.H. Sproule, from Baraboo, Wisconsin.

Pastor Sproule became interested in the baptism in the Holy Spirit through the Charles S. Price meetings in

137

The History of the FCA

Duluth, Minnesota. After personally receiving the baptism in the Holy Spirit, he led the congregation into accepting both the truth and experience of the Spirit-filled life. Thus, the first Pentecostal church in the city was underway.

As the group continued to grow, they moved from the mission to various halls for their gatherings. Then, during the Depression, their first building was built at 1925 Winnebago Street. They held the first services there on April 8, 1932. Sunday afternoon services were held and attracted many visitors who received Christ and were added to the church.

The congregation was shocked in 1937 by the sudden passing away of Pastor Sproule. Successive pastors since then have been: Mrs. W.H. Sproule, Rev. and Mrs. Ernest Ruff, Rev. Walter Guenther, Rev. Arthur Hauge (interim), Rev. Thomas E. Crane and Rev. Earl H. Browne, who remained until the summer of 1969. At that time, Rev. Browne resigned, and the church called Rev. and Mrs. Warren Heckman, who came in August 1969 and served until June 2002. Mitch and Cheri Milton then became pastors. John Ruck followed the Miltons. In December 2010, Lake City Church and Mad City Church merged, becoming City Church. Tom Flaherty, former pastor of Mad City Church, became the lead pastor. John Ruck became the associate pastor. The pastoral staff from both churches stayed on in their respective ministries.

LCC has grown consistently from a small group in 1969 to a mega church by 2002, moving from location to location as it grew, now on a 32-acre campus. In addition, it has helped in branching several additional local churches. It began a preschool daycare in 1977 that now has more than 350 children enrolled and a Christian school (K-12th grade) with more than 460 students enrolled.

Missionary outreach was a major ministry of LCC. An annual missions conference brought dozens of missionaries to LCC for encouragement and challenge.

Christian Hills Full Gospel Church
Westhaven, Illinois – 1928

Christian Hills began in 1928 as an independent church when a body of believers called Rev. Philip Wittich to pastor them. First services were held in the vacant Auburn Park Swedish Assembly, 70th and Elizabeth Streets, Chicago, Illinois, under the name Christ Church.

In 1932, the Orr College building at 6309 Yale Avenue was purchased. Services were held there until 1953, when the dedication of a new edifice at 9535 South Prospect Avenue was celebrated, as well as its 25th anniversary. It was at this time that the name was changed to Wittich Memorial in memory of the founder.

Upon the death of Pastor Wittich, Pastor Gordon P. Swartz was called in April of 1935 to be their pastor. Some 20 years later, the church purchased 40 acres at 159th and 91st Avenue, Westhaven, Illinois. On March 23, 1975, ground was broken for the erection of their present sanctuary, at which time the name was changed to

The History of the FCA

Christian Hills Full Gospel Church as the development on which the church rests was named Christian Hills. Dedication services were held on May 15, 1976. Pastor Swartz ministered at Christian Hills until his death on December 23, 1972.

On October 14, 1973, Pastor Osborn Arnes came to minister to the congregation and did so until 1992, at which time Pastor Jerry Sherstad became the senior pastor, followed by J.L. Rivera. Presently, Mike McCartney is the pastor.[42]

Friend Christian Assembly
Friend, Nebraska – 1931

Looking back to its earliest days, the promise of a church was born in cottage prayer meetings, some held in the home of Herbert Smith, the depot agent, and some led by Silas Miller, the pastor of a rural independent assembly near Milford, Nebraska.

In August 1931, Carl O. Johnson and his wife, Borghild, came to Friend with their four daughters, Marie, Eunice, Bernice and Norma. Since there was no place for them to move into, Amos and Edith May Eigsti and their 10 children opened their home, and the Johnsons lived with them for six weeks.

Later that year, a young evangelist named John Moseid came from Minnesota to Friend. A tent was set up on the property of John and Vilas Packard, and evangelistic meetings were held. Mrs. (Vilas) Packard was saved at that

Twenty-six

time and at age 85 is still attending the assembly (1992), the only one left of the group who committed their lives to the Lord in those meetings.

In that year, the vacant Baptist church located at Fifth and Chestnut was rented as a meeting place for the fledging church, and Friend Gospel Tabernacle had its first permanent home.

Those were severe drought years, and the church experienced difficult times. Sometimes it even appeared as if they may have to disband, but God had other plans for them.

They prayed earnestly that God would provide a church home they could call their own. But how? There were no funds, and no door seemed to open for them. Then one day while paying the rent, Pastor Johnson received a very pleasant surprise. Judge R.M. Proudfit, who had been taking care of the rent for the owners, announced to Brother Johnson that he and his wife had purchased the church property, and they had decided to donate it to the Friend Gospel Tabernacle congregation, absolutely free of debt. The people rejoiced and gave thanks! They had remained persistent in their faith and found that "… with God all things are possible" (Matthew 19:26).

The church prospered spiritually and became established in the community. In 1942, the pastor and board felt it was necessary to incorporate in the State of Nebraska. The men who signed and witnessed this special milestone for the assembly were Amos Eigsti, Willis

O'Neel, William B. Shafer, Carl O. Johnson and George B. Bouchard.

In April 1968, construction began on their present building. Building the church brought new understanding of the words cooperation, dedication and hard work! Both men and women gave as much time and strength as they were able to work on the structure. The dedication service was held on January 15, 1969, the highlight of several days of celebration.

The burning of the mortgage during the ministry of Rev. and Mrs. Gordon Fox in 1976 was another happy event for the congregation.

Rev. Carl O. Johnson, their first pastor, was followed by other faithful pastors. Through the years, the Lord called some from the congregation into full-time service. Mildred Eigsti, daughter of the Amos Eigstis, served in Liberia, West Africa, for 13½ years. Warren Heckman, the pastor of Lake City Church in Madison, Wisconsin, and Ronald Drake, pastor of Marquette Gospel Tabernacle, Marquette, Michigan, were called from the next generation of the membership. In the winter of 1990, the congregation had the joy of sending the Dan Burkeys to the Cornerstone Christian Assembly in Parker, Colorado, where he is serving as associate pastor.

Through the years, the congregation has been very active in sending forth and helping support many missionaries. In earlier years, when missionaries often depend upon barrels sent from the States, the congregation filled barrels with food and other needed supplies. Produce and meat from the farms of the members were canned by the ladies of the church. Garments were sewn for the mission children by these busy ladies and packed into the barrels along with the canned goods.

The old Baptist church building had no indoor plumbing. During Paul Johnson's ministry (1953-1956), the old basement was dug out, and restrooms and Sunday school rooms were added.

The church's first convention was held not too many years after becoming a church. Special speakers were John Moseid and E.O. Swanson. Other ministers attended. The meals were prepared at the church, much of the food being brought in from the farms and gardens.

During the years of the Percey Johnson ministry, a Ladies' Missionary Circle was begun.

During Pastor Matwichuk's ministry, Rev. and Mrs. Craig Fritzler served as youth pastors.

In November 1991, Pastor Kenneth Lundeen and his wife, Karon, daughter, Kim, and son, Kris, came from Balaton, Minnesota, to pastor. The following is a summary of the pastors who have served Friend Gospel Tabernacle over the years:

```
1931        First prayer meeting
1931-1937   Carl O. Johnson
1937-1939   Elfreda Ofstead
1940-1945   Carl O. Johnson
1945-1947   Arthur Rupp
```

The History of the FCA

1948-1949   Jacob Kocker
1949-1953   Percey Johnson
1956-1959   Gordon Scott
1960-1964   Wesley Braaten
1965-1971   Clinton Fick
1971-1975   Brian Hughes
1975-1977   Gordon Fox
1977-1984   Larry Matwichuk
1984-1991   Robert F. Kane
1991-2001   Kenneth G. Lundeen[43]
2002   Rod Brown
Present   Jerry Gill

Full Gospel Assembly
Hutchinson, Kansas – No year found

Rev. and Mrs. W.H. Sutliff and family moved to Hutchinson, Kansas, in 1922 from Belnap, Illinois. Accompanying them was a young couple, Noah and Bessie Krob, just recently married. They came to establish a new independent Pentecostal church. Rev. Sutliff's pioneering spirit and pastoral heart led him to begin a home Bible study. From this warm and comfortable environment, the church was born. The first service was held May 15, 1927. It is reported that Pastor Sutliff knew both Charles Parham and William Durham and attended their meetings.

From a very modest and unpretentious beginning, a sound, solid New Testament church was formed and

144

stayed alive with the Spirit of God. Though there have been many changes over the years, each one was a stepping stone. The goal and desire of the members and leadership of the assembly have always been the same — to see people saved by God's power and filled with the Holy Spirit and grow to full stature in the Lord.

For many years, the Full Gospel Assembly has been closely knit with the Fellowship of Christian Assemblies. However, the church has held its arms open to ministries of other Pentecostal groups. Rev. Sutliff's ministry and vision included a strong Sunday school and Saturday Bible school for youth and children. All through the years, world missions were emphasized, and several from the Assembly have gone into full-time Christian ministry. Rev. Sutliff served the church for 38 years.

Successive pastors have been Gordon Scott, Del Jester, Gordon Scott (second time), Brian Hughes, Bill Hobson, Brian Johnson, Al Wright and Gordon Scott (third time).[44]

Bethel Temple
St. Paul, Minnesota – No year found

Bethel Christian Fellowship, formerly Bethel Temple, was born out of the burden, prayer and vision that God gave to Mrs. Almeda M. Engquist in the spring of 1917 to start a church. Swedish born, Almeda and her husband, Charles, who owned a wholesale meat company, had been attending a Lutheran church before this.

A store at the corner of Snelling and Randolph became

Bethel's first home in 1927. Esther Wittner, a participant in the church from its beginning, remembered that "the power of the Lord" was present in such a way that people came from long distances, despite the Depression and travel time. You couldn't wait to go to the next service, he wrote. The Bethel Association was formally organized on August 19, 1930.

Sister Engquist led the regularly scheduled services, including a Tuesday morning prayer and praise meeting and a Sunday evening service that was aired over radio station WMIN. Sister Engquist preached the message, "Everything by Faith," and miraculous healings followed.

"Send a revival and save St. Paul" was the constant cry in the prayer meetings.

The believers bought eight lots at the corner of Snelling and Juno. A train coach was divided lengthwise in the middle and widened to make a building that would be large enough to hold 150 people. This new church home was dedicated on November 10, 1935, with Pastor J.E. Robinson of Oshkosh, Wisconsin, preaching in the afternoon and Pastor E.C. Erickson of Duluth, Minnesota, preaching in the evening. The crowd was too large for their building, and many had to be turned away.

Sister Engquist died in 1943. Charles, Almeda's husband, carried on as pastor for a time, involving numerous students from North Central Bible College, Minneapolis, Minnesota. A couple known as the Bergs and a Brother Solie helped during this time. Brother Engquist invited Paul and Myrtle Hild to serve as pastors, which they did during 1949 and 1950. Brother Engquist invited Evangelist Helen Jepsen to speak at Bethel in 1951. She stayed on for a while and was asked to remain as pastor.

Helen Jepsen was described as the "Tipple playing preacher of Bethel Temple." Born in Brookline, Massachusetts, she grew up in Boston. She had a praying mother but as a young woman was attracted to risqué performances and called herself a "Sahara, Oriental and Hula dancer" for clubs, stags and smokers. She and her sister, Ruth, traveled extensively, performing in many hotels across the land.

After being gloriously saved, she began traveling as an evangelist. Under her ministry, a church was born and thrived in Clarkfield, Minnesota.

During her years at Bethel, the church was strong in their emphasis on prayer, preaching, praise, healing, missions and faith. In 1957, they purchased the Second Church of Christ Scientist building at 1982 Iglehart with only a congregation of 33 people. It was dedicated on April 20, 1958 with Rev. E.C. Erickson from Duluth, Minnesota, speaking. Others participating were Roy Johnson, Seattle, Washington; Natalie Haag, Music Director at Calvary Temple (Soul's Harbor), Minneapolis, Minnesota; and Rev. Battle and his choir from St. Paul Gospel Temple.

When Sister Jepsen retired in 1969, Rev. Robert and Susan Forseth were called to pastor. They resigned in 1971, and Rev. Lloyd and Janna Jacobsen accepted the pastorate. The church grew through evangelism, bus ministry and multiple ministries. The seating capacity of 225 was no longer adequate. In October 1982, the congregation moved into the former Sons of Jacob Synagogue at 1466 Portland. During these years, many lay leaders were raised up, and four young men were ordained into the ministry: Rich Doebler, Jim Olson, Phil Tuttle and Joe Walsh.

In January 1989, Bethel bade farewell to the Jacobsens and welcomed as pastors Jim and Annette Olson, who continue to the present in serving Bethel as senior pastors.[45]

NOTE: Some of the dates in the above excerpts do not agree entirely with dates provided elsewhere in this book. This is apparently due to the reliance on people's memories rather than actual data; therefore, both dates have been included as the correct ones cannot be substantiated.

Twenty-seven
FCA Functioning Today

The 1980s and 1990s could be called times of transition for the FCA. For the most part, things changed rather drastically without an awareness of what was happening.

The founding fathers and early leaders of the Fellowship moved off the scene. Although they would have repudiated it, they were apostles among the churches of the Fellowship. They were followed because they were gifted leaders, not elected ones. Their churches and ministries thrived, their ideas worked and their lives evidenced the leading and anointing of the Holy Spirit. They led the way in branching new Fellowship churches, birthing foreign missions in new countries and speaking out for truth and against error. They were the primary speakers in conferences, both large and small. Their local churches hosted the big annual FCA conventions, and they spoke strongly for local church autonomy.

The Fellowship has become more democratized. Leadership is diffused, assignments are given to task forces, committees plan the annual international conventions, agendas are established and a chairman, parliamentarian and secretary selected for the business session. Fellowship Press, a voluntary cooperative corporation, has served the Fellowship in printing and publishing the magazine, *Fellowship Today*, since 1963. It ended with a smaller 6-page magazine called *FCA Leadership* taking its place, edited by Warren Heckman (the author of this book).

The fall Fellowship Concerns Convention meets for discussion, projection and recommendation to the annual spring FCA convention. The World Outreach Committee does basically the same. Committees seldom have the impact, motivation or passion that a strong individual leader has by simply leading the way in doing it. In the past, two or three large local churches were the pacesetters and their pastors recognized as leaders to be followed. In the mid-1990s, none of those men were alive, and their churches no longer have large leading congregations.

Several other churches of the FCA are now large aggressive assemblies with 500 to 2,500 people in Sunday morning attendance. However, their pastors have not stepped into the prominent place of trans-local church leadership positions.

Various reasons may be offered for this. First, they are uncomfortable being cast into this role. Second, they are consumed by the demands of leading thriving, growing local churches. Third, they are reluctant to lead, speak out and challenge tradition because of the inherent criticism that it brings. Fourth, they sense a change among their peers. There is a broader-based desire for all to speak their voice and each to do their own thing.

Author's Observation and Commentary

The following commentary comes from my up-front personal observations of the Fellowship of Christian Assemblies over the last half century. I'd like to preface them by stating that I strongly stand for the scriptural stance of the sovereignty of the local church. I do not believe we have to lose that independence in order to also stand strongly in supporting one another in systemic strategy and/or synergistic strength.

Systemic: The accentuating of interrelationships and the fact that one part of a system affects the whole. Not the same as the word systematic, which refers to how the system is ordered and organized.

Synergism: Joint action of discreet agencies in which the total effects is greater than the sum of their effects when acting independently, i.e. Biblically, one shall chase one thousand, but two can chase ten thousand.

In the beginning and during the early years, the FCA might be compared to a small local church. Everyone knew everyone by name, background, occupation, personality and gifts. What we do best is just get together on Sunday and sing, worship, pray, get inspired by the preaching and go home. Next Sunday, it is a repeat, and it is neat. Fellowship is sweet!

We don't organize activities. If they happen, they happen. If not, they don't. There aren't any extra ministries to administrate, orchestrate or things in which to participate. If coming to church on Sunday morning is not enough, then you are just coming to the wrong place for that other stuff!

And so in the FCA in an earlier day, everyone knew everyone. In both the annual national convention and in regional conferences, we gathered for worship, inspiration and fellowship. Good times, good friends and good preaching meant a good convention. Newcomers were few and far between, assimilated easily and without a ripple, becoming just like us without upsetting the apple cart. The occasional "young Turk" that rose up from among us, asking questions like "Why do we always do it like this, and why don't we try doing things like some other successful groups?" would soon feel put down and rejected. So lifting your voice and especially naming any other Pentecostal group in the United States was to carry a label and mark of suspicion for a long time. You could mention Scandinavian groups and their methods without rejection and ostracization, but not that their successful actions would be adopted. Regardless of the new idea, concept or suggestion, it usually met with euthanasia as prescribed by one of the proponents of the principles of the local church and it sovereignty.

The "young Turk" and the energetic, the creative and

Author's Observation and Commentary

the innovative, the frustrated and the forward thinkers had several choices. They could sit back and steam in their juices, frustrated to the boiling point, but remain quiet, grumbling under their breath. Or they could jump ship and join another group believed to be more progressive, open to change and following intentional group goals, objectives and purposes corporately. Another option was to slowly, continuously, carefully, prayerfully try to educate, agitate and activate new approaches, attitudes and actions. Finally, one could forget the Fellowship as far as this arena was concerned and simply throw yourself into making things happen within your ministry of the local church that you pastored. Conventions were faithfully attended; after all, your close friends were there, the preaching and fellowship were usually good and you experienced lots of inspiration and affirmation. If your church grew to be larger than most, you often were asked to speak and sit on various committees.

Within the FCA (then known as the Independent Assemblies of God), several pastors led their churches into large, thriving multi-ministry congregations. They were listened to, emulated, copied and followed by most of the other pastors and churches. They were each strong, fiercely independent and functioning successfully on their own. They saw little need to build stronger networking to help isolated, small, inadequate and sometimes incompetent local churches and pastors. Attempting to follow their lead, lesser ministries mouthed their main messages of local church sovereignty to their own hurt.

The History of the FCA

When attempts were made to discuss the possibility of an intentional, closer interdependence and support system among local churches and pastors, they were tabled, criticized or eventually curtailed.

Whoa! Now we are two, three or four times larger in number than just a few years ago, and I don't seem to know hardly anyone. What happened? Purposeful planning, goal setting, direction driven, cooperative commitment and intentional action sound denominationally directed and the beginning of sovereignty slippage! I'm not sure I like it this way. And some of these so-called Fellowship projects are a smokescreen to swallow up the sovereignty of the local church is my bet.

I may be wrong, but it is my idea and observation that this mode of thinking has often been the reaction of many of the older and younger FCA ministers through the years.

It is my opinion that we need to once again recognize, accept and listen to the leaders God has set among us, not by earthly electing, but by sovereign selecting. Otherwise, we are likely to fall prey to the maxim "When it's all said and done, more is said than done," and a minimum of cooperative effort, accomplishment and achievement will be the net result. Individual local churches will continue to grow and thrive, accomplishing great things, while others will diminish, dry up and disappear. Without direction and leadership in the local church, little is advanced or achieved, and it is the same collectively in the FCA.

Another comparison might be current terms used in

Author's Observation and Commentary

pastoring churches that grow beyond the 150 to 200-plus attendance mark. We are getting familiar with the words of moving from shepherd to rancher. The shepherd can only personally handle about that many sheep. To grow beyond that, he must become a rancher who operates with many foremen under his care who in turn give individual care to those under their care. Growth can continue indefinitely, and yet all are being cared for. The rancher can provide leadership, direction, inspiration, vision and equipping down through the ranks of his undershepherds. And he is free of fatigue and the exhaustion of overextension, thus able to move ahead in ministry to an ever-increasing ingathering.

Without this Biblical order and approach (like Moses and Jethro in Exodus 18), the good shepherd will work harder and longer until he collapses. In his weariness, he cannot keep up, think ahead, plan for the future or lead intentionally.

In the FCA, we have grown far beyond the ability to work successfully and cooperatively without leadership beyond local pastors. The early years of publishing the magazines *Herald of Faith* and later *Herald of Pentecost* in the 1930s, 1940s and 1950s demonstrate this principle. It was an overwhelming job for one local church and pastoral editor to maintain. It needed to become a cooperative Fellowship project, even to the organizing and incorporating and in having a paid managing editor, not a hardworking, willing local church pastor.

So we have the Fellowship Press Corporation of the

The History of the FCA

FCA, made up of local churches that voluntarily committed themselves to support this printing ministry financially on a monthly basis so that it would stay fiscally fit. Have they lost their local church sovereignty? Not for a minute! But they sacrificially and joyfully bless the whole Fellowship by their commitment to this cooperative endeavor. It is interesting to note that out of about 200 local churches now listed in the FCA Directory, only approximately 30 have chosen to join this nonprofit corporation and pay the price of putting it into their monthly budgets. All of the people in the local churches and the more than 500 FCA ministers benefit from the 30 churches bearing the burden of the budget, without losing either their cherished sovereignty or local church autonomy.

We face a similar situation with the World Outreach Committee and its future effectiveness. Let me use a little irony, satire and cynicism to spark your thoughtful response. As long as it was a quiet little committee bringing nice little reports to the annual convention, it was left to its own devices. But was the WOC satisfied? NO!

Now they want to organize, incorporate, administrate and dominate. They want to elect a Director! They want to subtly steal my sovereignty while saying they only want to serve! But I know better, and I'm against it and tell them, too!

Am I overstating the case? I hope so. Is this any different than our printing ministry via the auspices of Fellowship Press Corporation? A ministry outgrows

Author's Observation and Commentary

volunteerism; the potential is outstanding, yet without full-time leadership, it is stymied. For more than 10 years, we have heard about the possibilities of the WOC as reiterated in the test of the history of the WOC. At the annual convention, it is obvious from the WOC reports that busy pastors, who are working with this ministry, could not follow through on the probabilities during the past year because they were already overworked in their local churches. They didn't have the time, energy or resources.

To have an International Director, who could travel worldwide, visit local churches and visit our missionaries and mission stations, could put new vision, vitality and victory in the ranks. Coordinating cooperative outreaches, encouraging individual men and women in ministry, envisioning local churches, pastors and missionaries and inspiring trust, accountability, interaction and openness might give impetus to a revival of mission accomplishment through prayer, giving, recruitment and candidates.

The FCA is similar to a local church's softball team playing in a church league. But they aren't like other church teams in that they are unorganized. There really aren't any rules, plans, practices or procedures. Anyone can come, anyone can play and there are no requirements, no commitments and no costs. Come if you feel like it; you get to play, have your say and are allowed to stay.

Most other teams beat this team, but that is okay; we are just here for fun. Once in a while there are some stars that show up from within this church, but they do not last long. They usually end up joining another church team — doesn't seem like they are very loyal. On occasion, when leaving, they have said they wanted to be on a team that had a coach, regular practices, a plan of action and a goal in mind, but I think they were just hot dogs wanting to be somebody.

But as for us, we have just a bunch of good-time boys having a good time together down at the ballpark. It is true we win some, and we lose some. Nobody really keeps track — that's not why we get together. We enjoy one another, know one another and most of us have been getting together with one another for as long as we can remember. That's just the way it is. We aren't trying to be the major leagues, minor leagues or any league, for that matter. We don't want a coach telling us what to do, laying down rules, attendance requirements or fees to be paid. We like it just the way it is.

Through the years, church polity became a negative noose around our necks. Our edginess over indigenous, attack over autonomy and stubbornness over sovereignty have not always been Biblically based. On occasion, I believe these terms have been called forth to cover our ignorance, selfishness, laziness and rebelliousness. I don't mean for this to sound harsh and judgmental, but it is my personal observation. Case in point, true story; I was there.

In a national convention some years ago, we were discussing the challenge of planting new churches. A younger pastor suggested that someone with that gifting

Author's Observation and Commentary

and experience travel among the churches to raise monthly support for his family and the beginning expenses of birthing a new church. He hardly finished before one of our leading pastors of one of the larger churches cut him down to size for such a denominational idea, totally contrary to the sovereignty of the local church. Persisting, the young preacher said, "But, wait, isn't that what our missionaries do? If their own local church cannot fully support them, they itinerate among our churches until sufficient monthly support is raised, and then they head for the country of their calling."

With great condescension and exasperation, he was told, "That's different!" The constant cutting down of all cooperative concerns surely has contributed to some of our youngest, brightest and best leaving the FCA for what they hope will be greener pastures in another group open to change, creativity and corporate action.

There are so many positive things we could emphasize about the FCA. It is unity with diversity, freedom with accountability, purity and credibility, opportunity for ministry, larger-than-average-per-capita number of growing churches, friendship, warmth, number of missionaries, fellowship, love, bonding, inspiration, strong missions outreach and positive changes underway. The FCA is not a top-heavy, restrictive organization, controlling every move, stipulating not suggesting what you must support, insisting not inviting you to be involved, legislating a levy, like it or not, and crushing your creativity. There is very little or no politics because there are not positions on the organizational ladders to climb, offices to strive for or places in which you can become a power broker.

Unquestionably more people are attracted to the positive than to the negative. I believe our critical, cynical, negative and defensive anti-stance of the past is slowly and more or less quietly being left behind. I sense a longing among us to look forward to new cooperative concepts that network us together.

I believe our cooperative ventures of the future have great promise. Proactive, intentional and creative planning are the format of the day, not reactive, regressive and rejective responses. In our desire to remain autonomous local churches, we must be open to scriptural synergy without losing sovereignty. There is much to learn from other likeminded groups who have walked this path before us.

Multiple church historians have charted the life and times of a given movement in these terse terms:

1. Revitalize
2. Evangelize
3. Organize
4. Fossilize
5. Apostatize

I share a healthy concern in not wanting that to happen to the FCA.

Conclusion

History is always intriguing. There is far more to it than meets the eye. There are significant facts, figures and forces that are overlooked, some consciously and some unconsciously. Decisions, decisions! What should be included? I wrote it from my own biased perspective, even though I have tried to be objective. My own history has shaped my attitudes and actions.

I have tried to give a reasonable account of the history of our group of pastors and local churches in this book. I hope that it will be helpful to this generation's understanding of who we are and where we have come from. In addition, it is my hope that it will add meaning to our insistence on the autonomy of the local church. I pray that it will inspire us to actively investigate our great opportunities of involvement interdependently.

Appendices

FCA Statement
of Mission and Beliefs

After many years of study and discussion, finally in 1986 at the joint USA/Canadian FCA Annual Convention in Banff, Alberta, Canada, "A Statement of Nature and Mission and Common Beliefs" was adopted:

> We are a fellowship of autonomous, evangelical churches with historical roots within the Pentecostal movement. We view ourselves as called of God to share in mutual Christian care and practical cooperation in carrying out the Great Commission of our Lord Jesus Christ. We affirm our commitment to both local church autonomy and interchurch cooperation as Biblical norms for our life and ministry. We also affirm our call to work in the spirit of love and unity with all true believers in our common ministry within the Kingdom of God.

Our Statement of Beliefs was basically a standard evangelical doctrinal statement, with conservative additions regarding the sovereignty of the local church and acceptance of the Pentecostal baptism in the Holy Spirit, gifts and empowering of the church for its work, life and worship.

The History of the FCA

They have been published since that time in each issue of *Fellowship Today* magazine.

We believe:

- The Bible to be the only inspired, infallible and authoritative Word of God (John 16:13, II Timothy 3:15-17, II Peter 2:21, I Thessalonians 2:13)

- That there is one God, eternally existent in three persons, Father, Son and Holy Spirit (Deuteronomy 6:4, Isaiah 43:10-11, Matthew 28:19, Luke 3:22, John 14:16)

- In the deity of our Lord Jesus Christ (John 1:1, 14; 20:28-29, Philippians 2:6-11, Isaiah 9:6, Colossians 2:9)

- His virgin birth (Matthew 1:18, Luke 1:34-35, Isaiah 7:14)

- His sinless life (II Corinthians 5:21, Hebrews 4:15; 7:26-27, I John 3:5, I Peter 2:22)

- His miracles (Matthew 4:23, Luke 6:17-19, John 3:2)

- His vicarious and atoning death through His shed blood (Colossians 1:14, 20, Romans 5:8-9, Ephesians 1:7)

- His bodily resurrection (I Corinthians 15:3-4, Luke 24:4-7; 36-48, Revelation 1:17-18)

Appendices

- His ascension to the right hand of the Father (Acts 2:33; 5:30-31, I Peter 3:22)

- His personal return in power and glory (Acts 1:11, Philippians 2:9-11, I Thessalonians 1:10; 4:13-18, John 14:1-3)

- That justification by faith in the atonement of Jesus Christ and regeneration by the Holy Spirit is absolutely essential for the salvation of lost and sinful man (Romans 3:24-25, John 3:3-7, I John 5:11-13, Ephesians 2:1-16, Revelation 5:9, Acts 4:12, I Corinthians 6:11)

- The prime agency for the Word of God's Kingdom is the Christian local church functioning under the sovereignty of our Lord Jesus Christ. To the church have been entrusted the ordinances of believer's baptism and the Lord's Supper (Acts 2:41-47; 16:4-5, Matthew 16:18; 28:18-20, Ephesians 1:22-23, I Corinthians 12, I Corinthians 11:23-26)

- In the present ministry of the Holy Spirit, which includes: the baptism in the Holy Spirit as an experience distinct from regeneration; His indwelling by which the Christian is enabled to live a godly life; His supernatural gifting and empowering of the church for its work, life and worship (Luke 24:49, Acts 1:4-8; 2:1-4; 10:44-46, I Corinthians 12, 14)

- In the return of Jesus Christ to consummate His Kingdom in the resurrection of both the saved and the lost, those who are saved unto the resurrection of life and those who are lost unto the resurrection of damnation (John 5:28-29, Mark 14:62, II Thessalonians 1:2-10, Revelation 1:5-7; 20:4-5, 11-12)

- In the spiritual unity of believers in our Lord Jesus Christ (John 17:11, 21-23, Romans 12:4-4, Ephesians 4:11-16)

Directory of Ministers

Over the years, the ministerial listing process was updated, strengthened and clarified repeatedly. Excerpts from various national convention business sessions read as follows:

> Persons desiring to be listed should secure recommendations of two fellowshipping pastors, preferably in their general area, and space for this should be provided on the application form. A local home church should be listed for each person desiring to be listed. The listing of various associations in lieu of a home church is held to be in variance with our convictions.

Emphasis on the local church is an ongoing theme. A common question for identification and credibility is, "What local church do you belong to, and are you in good standing with it?" Secondly, "Are you in good standing with your pastor and the elders of your local church?" "Can they and will they give you a good recommendation morally, ethically, doctrinally, financially and in regards to your family?" These questions are not asked of the FCA at large, but of the person's local church and pastor.

Fellowship of Christian Assemblies Minister's Application for Listing New Members

TYPE OR PRINT NEATLY:
(MUST BE RETURNED BY DECEMBER 15)

Name: _____

      Last   First   Initial

Home Phone: _____

Spouse: _____

      Last   First   Initial

Home Address: _____

      Street/P.O.

_____

  City   State   Zip

Missionary Field Address: _____

_____

Appendices

Applicant's marital status: ( ) Married ( ) Divorced ( ) Single
( ) Widowed   ( ) Remarried

At/From the following church: _____

Church Phone: _____

Your Title: _____

Specify preferred mailing address:

_____

I am a member of the following church:

_____

Address of the Church:

_____
Street/P.O.   City   State   Zip

I was ( ) ordained ( ) Licensed by: _____ Date: _____

Are you presently listed with any other regional or national
association of ministers or churches? ( ) Yes ( ) No

The History of the FCA

Please have two ministers from the Fellowship sign their endorsement below. Please include a fee of $50.00, which includes your listing, one copy of the Directory and subscriptions to *Fellowship Today* and *Pursuit.*

Make payable to: Fellowship Directory
Mail to: FCA City Church, c/o Nancy Van Maren, 4909 E. Buckeye Rd, Madison, WI 53716

We, the undersigned, recommend this new applicant for listing in the Fellowship of Christian Assemblies Directory. On the basis of our knowledge of his life and ministry, we believe him/her to be worthy of our wholehearted Christian Fellowship.

_____

Signature (Printed and written)

_____

Signature (Printed and written)

Notes from record or proceedings of national gatherings, 1965 and 1966:
"Persons desiring to be listed should secure recommendations of two fellowshipping pastors, preferably in his general area, and space for this should be provided on the application form. A local home church should be listed for each person desiring to be listed. The listing of various associations in lieu of a home church is held to be in variance with our convictions."

The information contained in this Directory is provided as a ministry to the Fellowship of Christian Assemblies and is based upon responses received from individuals and churches within the FCA. No

Appendices

independent verification has been made of the accuracy or completeness of the responses received; therefore, neither of us in Madison, Wisconsin, nor the FCA assumes responsibility for errors or omissions in compilation and publication of this Directory.

The Biblical principle of Acts 9:26-30 is important in authenticating new ministers in the FCA. Barnabus recommended newly converted Saul of Tarsus to the church at Jerusalem. There is a deep continuous desire that surfaces repeatedly: first, to always adhere to Biblical principles of morality, integrity and doctrinal purity for those serving in ministry; and, second, to allow for the sovereignty of each local church in determining and interpreting those truths, with regards to whom can be listed or needs to be deleted from the annual FCA Directory. Thus we have an incredible challenge to maintain a credible listing each year.

Fellowship of Christian Assemblies
Request Form for Church Listing

In order for a church to be listed in the Directory of the Fellowship of Christian Assemblies, this form must be completed in full and returned to us no later than December 15. Please include a listing fee of $150.00. Copies of the Directory are an additional $10.00 each.

Church Name: _____

Address: _____

Church Telephone: _____

Church Fax: _____

Pastor: _____

Staff: _____   _____
　　　　　(Full Name)　　　　　　　　(Title or position)

　　　　_____   _____

　　　　_____   _____

　　　　_____   _____

Appendices

Missionaries (only those being "sent" from this church):

_____   _____
(Full Name)   (Country)

_____   _____

_____   _____

_____
Signature (Printed and written) FCA Member requesting listing

_____
Signature (Printed and written) Authorized Church representative

Date: _____

Please make check payable to: Fellowship Directory
Mail to: FCA City Church, c/o Nancy Van Maren, 4909 E. Buckeye
Rd, Madison, WI 53716

The applications for listing by missionaries who are out of the country
are either faxed to them for their signatures or signed for them by the
respective churches that sent them out.

Local Church Principles
From the FCA Handbook

The Fellowship holds the view that the New Testament scriptures illustrate the basic principles of church life and practice, including the autonomy of the local congregation.

While scholarship widely recognizes that the New Testament presents no authoritative organization above the local church during the apostolic era, we maintain further that this basic autonomous church life portrayed in the New Testament is beneficial for all ages of the church.

Local church autonomy is not an end in itself. Our first concern is the sovereign freedom of the Lord Jesus Christ to act in His churches through the Word and the Spirit. We hold that this freedom of God is enhanced in the context of the freedom of the congregation from external religious authority.

We also hold that local church autonomy reinforces the concept of the unity of the Body of Christ. Each congregation is an expression of that body, functioning under the leadership of Christ.

The New Testament is concerned with church organization and orderly functioning, focusing upon one basic area, the local church. Believers gathered for worship, fellowship, care and service in the local assembly.

Appendices

Here elected or appointed special ministries were carried out, and discipline was practiced. Christian workers were ordained and sent by the local church. Churches were nourished in the truth that they lived and served under the sovereignty of Jesus Christ. (See Ephesians 1:20-22; 4:15-16, Colossians 1:15-18.)

Ministers of the Gospel were directly related to the local home churches. The accountability of Peter to the church at Jerusalem and the accountability of Paul and Barnabas to the church at Antioch are examples of the close relationship of ministers to their home assemblies. (See Acts 11:1-18; 14:1-3; 14:26-28.)

We view the conference of Acts 15 as an event that primarily concerned two local churches, although its results were of instruction and blessing to other assemblies in a voluntary, non-binding manner.

In each church, duly appointed or elected leaders — elders, deacons and deaconesses — were servants and overseers with responsibility for the spiritual and temporal care of the congregation. (See Philippians 1:1, I Timothy 3:1-13, I Peter 5:1-4, Acts 6:1-6; 20:17-35.)

The New Testament, although portraying no organic union of churches, does reveal a spiritual fellowship and voluntary cooperation among the assemblies. This is illustrated especially by the cooperative efforts of the Gentile churches in sending relief to the impoverished churches of Judea. (See II Corinthians 8-9, Romans 15:25-27.) This intentional, united project is sufficient to point to the fact that churches of the New Testament era were not isolated and hyper-independent. The freedom of the Lord Jesus Christ to act within the congregation through the Word and the Spirit was also a freedom to act in loving, practical concern for other congregations, thus demonstrating the unity of the Body of Christ.

We realize that this whole concept places upon local church leadership a great responsibility to develop in the congregation responsiveness to the authority of the scriptures and the leading of the Spirit. Autonomy should not lead to carnal local church authority.

We also recognize that congregational autonomy, although aiming at church health, does not in itself guarantee such wellbeing. We do believe it provides a normal, scriptural seed bed for developing assemblies responsive to the Lordship of Christ as He calls us to the life and work of the Great Commission.

We make no exclusive claims concerning our concepts of local church and interchurch life, recognizing that similar views have been held by many others within the longstanding "free church" tradition. We also recognize the freedom of God to act in His will and grace in the context of various forms of church polity.

Cooperative Procedures From the FCA Handbook

The Fellowship, although unincorporated, has developed specific means for recognizing ministers and churches as active participants. It is an identifiable family — with identifiable forms of cooperative effort, which are described in this section.

A Family of Ministers and Churches

New ministers and churches are recognized by the Fellowship at large by virtue of their having entered into cooperative fellowship locally and regionally with other churches and ministers of the FCA. This local and regional recognition is largely informal and relational.

Local pastors and churches become accountable for the character and integrity of those whom they introduce to the Fellowship. (See Acts 9:26-28.)

Formal recognition on a Fellowship-wide basis comes through listing in the annual Fellowship Directory. Details of this process were described earlier.

The Fellowship is constantly pursuing Biblical and practical ways to enhance and strengthen inter-ministerial accountability within our local church polity.

The Fellowship Directory does not define the boundaries of the Fellowship precisely since some active participants may not yet be listed, and others failed to get their annual applications sent in.[35]

Resource Materials

1. *Pentecostal Evangel*, The General Council of the Assemblies of God, Springfield, MO, November 16, 1989, p. 3.
2. Stanley M. Burgess and Gary B. McGee, *Dictionary of Pentecostal and Charismatic Movements*, Regency/Zondervan Publishing House, Grand Rapids, MI, 1988, pp. 811-829.
3. Thomas G. Wilson, *Paraclete*, Gospel Publishing House, Springfield, MO, Spring, 1990, p. 12, quoting Dr. Richard W. Bishop, "Power Evangelism Today," Global Church Growth 25, Oct.-Dec., 1988.
4. Vinson Synan, *Paraclete*, Gospel Publishing House, Springfield, MO, Fall, 1989, p. 1, quoting Donald Dayton, *The Theological Roots of Pentecostalism*, Francis Asbury Press, Grand Rapids, MI, 1987.
5. Daniel G. Reid, *Dictionary of Christianity in America*, InterVarsity Press, Downers Grove, IL, 1990, pp. 540-541.
6. Vinson Synan, *In the Latter Days*, Servant Books, Ann Arbor, MI, 1984, p. 36.
7. Ibid, pp. 37-38.
8. Mark A. Noll, *Eerdmans' Handbook to Christianity in America*, Wm. B. Eerdmans Publishing Co., Grand Rapids, MI, 1983, pp. 331-339.
9. Ibid, p. 334.

The History of the FCA

10. Daniel G. Reid, *Dictionary of Christianity in America*, InterVarsity Press, Downers Grove, IL, 1990, p. 882.

11. Stanley M. Burgess and Gary B. McGee, *Dictionary of Pentecostal and Charismatic Movements*, Regency/Zondervan Publishing House, Grand Rapids, MI, 1988, p. 255.

12. Henry Jauhiainen, Lecture "History of the FCA," FCA National Convention, Edmonton, Alberta, Canada, April, 1990.

13. Stanley M. Burgess and Gary B. McGee, *Dictionary of Pentecostal and Charismatic Movements*, Regency/Zondervan Publishing House, Grand Rapids, MI, 1988, pp. 255-256.

14. Russell Doebler, *A History of the Fellowship of Christian Assemblies*, Unpublished, 1986, p. 14, quoting from William Durham, *Organization*, Elbethel Christian work, Chicago, IL, January/March, 1950, p. 208.

15. Stanley M. Burgess and Gary B. McGee, *Dictionary of Pentecostal and Charismatic Movements*, Regency/Zondervan Publishing House, Grand Rapids, MI, 1988, p. 308.

16. Henry Jauhiainen, Lecture "History of the FCA," FCA National Convention, Edmonton, Alberta, Canada, April, 1990.

17. *Herald of Pentecost*, Duluth Gospel Tabernacle, Duluth, MN, May, 1953, p. 9.

18. Stanley M. Burgess and Gary B. McGee, *Dictionary of Pentecostal and Charismatic Movements*, Regency/

Appendices

Zondervan Publishing House, Grand Rapids, MI, 1988, p. 263.

19. Henry Jauhiainen, Lecture "History of the FCA," FCA National Convention, Edmonton, Alberta, Canada, April, 1990.

20. Stanley M. Burgess and Gary B. McGee, *Dictionary of Pentecostal and Charismatic Movements*, Regency/ Zondervan Publishing House, Grand Rapids, MI, 1988, p. 263.

21. Henry Jauhiainen, Lecture "History of the FCA," FCA National Convention, Edmonton, Alberta, Canada, April, 1990.

22. Ibid.

23. *Herald of Faith*, Volume One, Number One, Duluth Gospel Tabernacle, Duluth, MN, January, 1936, p. 3.

24. Henry Jauhiainen, Lecture "History of the FCA," FCA National Convention, Edmonton, Alberta, Canada, April, 1990.

25. Ibid.

26. Stanley M. Burgess and Gary B. McGee, *Dictionary of Pentecostal and Charismatic Movements*, Regency/ Zondervan Publishing House, Grand Rapids, MI, 1988, pp. 711-712.

27. Henry Jauhiainen, Lecture "History of the FCA," FCA National Convention, Edmonton, Alberta, Canada, April, 1990.

28. Ibid.

29. *Herald of Pentecost*, Duluth Gospel Tabernacle, Duluth, MN, March, 1956, p. 1.

30. Duluth Gospel Tabernacle, Diamond Jubilee Booklet — 1916-1976, "Highlights of History," Duluth Gospel Tabernacle, Duluth, MN, August, 1976, p. 5.

31. Henry Jauhiainen, Lecture "History of the FCA," FCA National Convention, Edmonton, Alberta, Canada, April, 1990.

32. *Herald of Faith*, Duluth Gospel Tabernacle, Duluth, MN, August, 1946, p. 15.

33. Lloyd Jacobsen, *Fellowship Today*, Fellowship Press, Seattle, WA, July, 1989, p. 4.

34. *Conviction*, Fellowship Press, Seattle, WA, April, 1986, p. 5.

35. Henry Jauhiainen and Richard Doebler, *Fellowship of Christian Assemblies Handbook*, Philadelphia Press, Seattle, WA, 1992, pp. 8-15.

36. Philadelphia Church, *1901-1986 — 85ᵗʰ Anniversary — A Brief History*, Philadelphia Press, Seattle, WA, 1986, pp. 1-13.

37. Karl Tongedahl, *A Brief History of Bethel Christian Assembly (1906-1989)*, Bethel Christian Assembly, Tacoma, WA, 1991, p. 1.

38. Albin Anderson, Pearl Nybakken, Harold A. Spong and Ruth Wiener, *Lake View Gospel Church History*, Lake View Gospel Church, Chicago, IL, October, 1989, pp. 6-9.

39. *Homewood Full Gospel Church Pictorial Directory*, Homewood Full Gospel Church, Homewood, IL, 1993, p. 2.

40. *Diamond Jubilee — Duluth Gospel Tabernacle,*

Appendices

Duluth Gospel Tabernacle, Duluth, MN, 1976, pp. 5-28.

41. *Philadelphia Church 35th Anniversary*, Philadelphia Church, Chicago, IL, 1961, pp. 1-11.

42. *Dedication of Our New Church*, Christian Hills Full Gospel Church, Orland Hills, IL, May 15, 1976, pp. 1-10.

43. 60-Year Celebration Brochure, Friend Christian Assembly, Friend, NE, 1992, pp. 1-8.

44. 60th Anniversary Celebration Booklet, Full Gospel Assembly, Hutchinson, KS, May 16, 1987, pp. 1-11.

45. Ken Holmgren, *Sixty Years at Bethel Christian Fellowship*, Bethel Christian Fellowship, St. Paul, MN, November, 1990, pp. 1-10.

About the Author

Dr. Warren has been married to and in active ministry with his wife, Donna, for 52 years. They have traveled extensively in the United States, Canada, Mexico, Africa, Argentina, Uruguay, Ecuador, Bolivia, Spain, Ukraine, Latvia, India and Belize, ministering in churches, conferences and Bible colleges and conducting marriage seminars.

They pastored in Nebraska and Minnesota before going to Madison, Wisconsin, in 1969, where they pastored for 33 years. The church grew from a small group of people to more than 1,100 on Sunday mornings worshipping together. They planted six new churches and helped start many others. They began a preschool/daycare that grew to about 400 in attendance and a K-12th grade Christian school that grew to about 500 in attendance. The buildings housing these ministries encompassed more than 130,000 square feet on a 32-acre campus.

The Heckmans' ministry features a strong Biblical emphasis, focusing on balanced, practical Christian living, the priority of the home, a positive productive faith in Christ, disciplined growth in the fullness of the Spirit, the central role of the local church and living a life of victory, joy and fulfillment in service of Christ and community.

They have three grown married children, all serving in full-time ministry, and six grandchildren. The Heckmans have experienced many of the joys and sorrows that a life of ministry, marriage and family can bring. Through it all they have maintained a positive attitude, a passion for Jesus, the local church and a passion for each other.

Pastor Heckman presently serves as the Fellowship of Christian Assemblies national coordinator, traveling the world visiting FCA missionaries and United States and Canada FCA churches on a halftime basis, helping, counseling, encouraging, preaching and mentoring.

The History of the

Fellowship of Christian Assemblies

is published by Good Book Publishing

www.goodbookpublishing.com

a division of Good Catch Publishing.

To find out how to publish the inspirational

and evangelical dramatic stories of members

in your church, or read others' stories, go to:

Good Catch Publishing at

www.goodcatchpublishing.com.